Hormonal Imbalance

THE MADNESS AND THE MESSAGE

by Terry Dorian, Ph.D.

Huntington House Publishers

Unless otherwise indicated, Scripture quotations are taken
from the HOLY BIBLE, NEW INTERNATIONAL
VERSION. Copyright © 1973, 1978, 1984 by
International Bible Society.
Used by permission of Zondervan Publishing House.

Scripture quotations marked (NLT) are taken from the
HOLY BIBLE, NEW LIVING TRANSLATION
Copyright © 1996. Used by permission of
Tyndale House Publishers, Inc.
Wheaton, Illinois 60189. All rights reserved.

Huntington House Publishers
P.O. Box 53788
Lafayette, Louisiana 70505

Library of Congress Card Catalog Number 98-75709
ISBN 1-56384-156-8

The theories and research represented here are based on
the author's study and experience. Readers should consult a
competent medical doctor and/or a highly trained and licensed
holistic health practitioner before adopting the therapeutic ap-
plications in this book. The author and publisher disclaim any
liability arising directly or indirectly from the use of this book.

Dedication

John R. Lee, M.D.
who has helped women across our nation and throughout
the world achieve optimal health and hormonal balance by
offering us information our physicians would not, or could
not, give us.

David T. Zava, Ph.D.
whose work in biomedical research offers vital information
to all of us seeking to understand the causes of and cures
for hormonal imbalance.

Medical Doctors and Holistic Health Practitioners
who have purposed to become lifelong learners in order
to assist and instruct men, women, and children who seek
help in overcoming the ravages of infectious and
degenerative disease.

Stan Bynum and Khem Shahani, Ph.D.
who support an interdisciplinary approach to the
study of health and nutrition,
and

Educated Consumers
who recognize the vital ways in which the work in many
academic disciplines (e.g., food science and technology,
biochemistry, clinical nutrition, epidemiology, culinary
history, cultural anthropology, religion, and medicine)
contributes to our understanding of optimal
health and well-being.

About the Author

Terry Dorian, Ph.D., and Her Mission

As a health researcher and organic whole foods advocate for over twenty-five years, Terry Dorian pays particular attention to the clinical and epidemiological studies connecting dietary and lifestyle habits and disease. While she supports the vital role of nutritional supplementation in overcoming degenerative disease, her message is clear: whole foods (preferably organic) lay the foundation for optimal health. Her current inquiry focuses on the measurable ways in which naturally occurring substances in foods affect physiologic processes. Clearly, the therapeutic benefits of nutraceuticals, isolated nutrients, herbal formulations, friendly microorganisms (probiotics), and digestive enzymes are optimized when used in conjunction with an optimal diet consisting of whole foods.

Dr. Dorian argues that those who speak and write on the topic of wellness, and on the therapeutic benefits of nutritional products, must regard the study of health and nutrition as an interdisciplinary effort. Those who offer advice and information concerning the prevention and cure of degenerative disease cannot meet the needs of consumers without taking into account the research being done in a number of academic disciplines. Subject areas that are particularly relevant to the study of optimal health and nutrition are food science and technology, biochemistry, culinary history, cultural anthropology, epidemiology, clinical nutrition, exercise physiology, psychology, religion, and medicine (to name a few).

Terry Dorian considers a liberal arts education a requisite for evaluating the weight and worth of the conclusions reached by various experts who have received specialized training in any one of a number of academic disciplines. Her own areas of training at the doctoral level are Aristotelian rhetoric (encompassing all available means of persuasion) and argumentation. Dr. Dorian draws on these skills in evaluating the credibility and pertinence of research related to health and nutrition. She finds her training in rhetoric particularly helpful in recognizing the obstacles that consumers face in finding the will and wisdom to achieve optimal health. We cannot find the will and wisdom to walk in wellness without asking the most elementary questions: who are the healthiest people in the world—and why? Who are the world leaders in degenerative disease, and what can those people do to achieve optimal health and fitness? We cannot answer those questions meaningfully, or completely, without attending to relevant, and indeed vital, research being done in a wide range of academic disciplines.

Terry Dorian believes that the best teachers (of health or any other topic) are the best students, lifelong learners whose mindfulness impacts the lives of others.

> The substance of liberal education appears to consist in the recognition of basic problems, in knowledge of distinctions and interrelations in subject matter, and in the comprehension of ideas. . . . The liberally educated man understands, by understanding the distinctions and interrelations of the basic fields of subject matter, the differences and connections between poetry and history, science and philosophy, theoretical and practical science; he understands that the same methods cannot be applied in all these fields; he knows the methods appropriate to each. . . . The liberally educated man has a mind that can operate well in all fields. He may be a specialist in one field. But he can understand anything important that is said in any field and can see and use the light that it sheds upon his own.

Robert Maynard Hutchins, *The Great Conversation: The Substance of a Liberal Education,* vol. 1 of *Great Books of the Western World* (Chicago: University of Chicago, 1952), 3-4.

As a consumer advocate, Terry Dorian urges those who seek wellness to acknowledge the scope of the inquiry regarding health and nutrition and to become lifelong learners. Only those who are educated consumers can demand competence from those who claim that they are qualified to treat disease. All licensed health practitioners ought to recognize the limitations of their own areas of specialization. They should also acknowledge, and examine whenever possible, those widely available research studies that offer hope to all of us who are interested in the prevention and cure of disease. Educated consumers should encourage the development of sustainable agriculture and support dietary guidelines based on scientific research rather than on market interests. Responsible, educated consumers continue to study the nutritional and therapeutic value of whole foods and the appropriate use of nutritional supplements, whole food concentrates, nutraceuticals, and herbal formulations.

With Gratitude

To my family and friends
who strengthen and encourage me
and whose gifts of time and talent
facilitate all that I do.

To my husband, Gary
whose very being
assures me of
God's presence, peace,
and discipline
in my life.

To our Lord
who is faithful and merciful and
who promises that all things are possible
in Him.

Contents

———————————————————————— Part One

What Is the
Madness and the Message?

The Scope and Nature of the Madness

1. The Madness is our ignorance as a people concerning the meaning and necessity of whole foods in sustaining life.

2. The Madness is the corruption of our government in areas that directly impact our health and well-being.

3. The Madness is the duplicity of those in authority at many of our medical schools: those in leadership watch silently as life-saving information is ignored and vital studies go unheralded. The Madness is the fact that "Medical research is dependent on the $billions of grants from the National Institutes of Health (NIH) and the private pharmaceutical industry."[1]

4. The Madness is mainstream print and electronic media that bury wisdom, knowledge, and truth by routinely glutting consumers with information designed to serve business interests.

5. The Madness is the widespread acceptance of life-threatening prescription drugs and synthetic hormones as treatments for the symptoms of degeneration, an unwillingness to seek and understand the causes of physical degeneration, and the maniacal indifference to the safe, healthy, and available solutions to hormonal imbalance.

6. The Madness is the widespread ignorance concerning xenobiotics. Very few people understand the ways in which these petrochemical derivatives impact the health of every man, woman, and child in the industrialized world. Very few people have the information that they need in order to limit their exposure to these foreign hormones; very few people understand the connection between hormone mimics and hormonal imbalance.

Putting the Madness in Perspective:

> Evil men do not understand justice,
>   but those who seek the LORD understand it fully.
>
> Proverbs 28:5

> Better a poor man whose walk is blameless
>   than a rich man whose ways are perverse.
>
> Proverbs 28:6

> Fear of man will prove to be a snare,
>   but whoever trusts in the LORD is kept safe.
>
> Proverbs 29:25

> The righteous detest the dishonest;
>   the wicked detest the upright.
>
> Proverbs 29:27

> When you sit to dine with a ruler,
>   note well what is before you,
> and put a knife to your throat
>   if you are given to gluttony.
> Do not crave his delicacies,
>   for that food is deceptive.
>
> Proverbs 23:1-3

We are not powerless. Fear, anger, bitterness, unforgiveness, and despair are crippling. But faith causes us to seek truth, to embrace it, and to share it with those we meet. Faith changes our lives and by faith we change the world—one person at a time. But we must be honest before the Lord, conscious of our failures, our limitations, and our self interests. Taking care of our bodies is our responsibility in Christ. We are His, bought with a price, and temples of the Holy Spirit.

We cannot take care of our bodies if we disregard the very provision that God has made for us. A great many people are awakening to knowledge concerning the healing power of food. The list of phytochemicals found in plants is an ever unfolding wonder. The ways in which vitamins, minerals, enzymes, antioxidants, essential fatty acids, and phytonutrients maintain and restore our bodies ought to make us stand in awe of God's provision for our physical health and well-being.

We cannot ignore the land on which we depend for life and sustenance, and expect to prosper. Because we are no longer an agrarian economy, we imagine that we may ignore the land without suffering consequences. Most of us simply expect other people to produce food to meet our needs. Moreover, most people in our country do not concern themselves with how food is grown or with who grows it. And, yet, that should be one of our greatest concerns. The methods of farming that have been in practice in the United States since World War II have contributed greatly to the degeneration of our physical bodies. Farming practices have depleted the soil of vital nutrients.

A move to prevent consumers from determining which food is fit to eat reached a crisis this year (1998) as we battled to maintain honest labeling for organic food. Tens of thousands of us signed petitions, made phone calls, and wrote letters in an effort to preserve the integrity of the organic label in order that we might continue to select food that is safe to consume!

> WASHINGTON, May 8—Bowing to the wishes of consumers, the Government announced today that it would not allow food to be labeled "organic" if it was genetically engineered, irradiated or grown in soil fertilized with sewage sludge.[2]

The Organic Trade Association represents eight hundred companies that grow and sell organic food. We must be thankful that a number of people are interested in growing and selling food that is not only free from contamination, but which contains the nutrients that ought to be present in nutrient-rich soil. However, the battle to maintain the integrity of organic labeling is not over.

Most people in America have not walked through a field of grain. Certainly our government schools do not teach the value of organic farming and sustainable agriculture. At the very least, we can ask our grocers for organic produce and ask for the certification papers which confirm that the products we seek are indeed organically grown. The next step is to write or call the certification organizations and ask them how they determine whether or not a product receives certification. What requirements do they make concerning land use and growing methods? If we no longer have the time or the inclination to work the land, we must surely concern ourselves with the availability of a safe and nutrient-rich supply of grains, beans, fruit, and vegetables.

But this is the United States, and we are approaching the year 2000. Most Americans do not eat grains (intact), legumes, fresh fruit, and vegetables on a regular basis or in sufficient quantities. Few people consider it their responsibility to pay attention to the standards of those companies and individuals that grow our food. The Word of God indicates that we must concern ourselves with working the land or suffer loss.

> He who works his land will have abundant food,
>   but he who chases fantasies lacks judgment.
>   Proverbs 12:11

> He who works his land will have abundant food,
>   but the one who chases fantasies will have his fill of
>   poverty.
>   Proverbs 28:19

We have supermarkets with rows and rows of bread-like products made from devitalized flour, which has been stripped of 98 percent of the natural nutrients found in the germ of the wheat berry and robbed of the essential fatty acids. The manufacturers, distributors, and retailers of processed, devitalized foods deliver to us an abundance and a variety of products that lack all that is essential for optimal health and nutrition—at what we perceive to be a low price. The epidemiological studies are conclusive. There is a clear connection between the rate of degenerative disease and dietary habits.[3] Cheap and tasty processed and devitalized grain-based products, laden with chemicals and additives, are abundant. Animal products filled with synthetic hormones and antibiotics are plentiful. The dietary regimen of most Americans features food high in animal fat and refined vegetable oil, high in sugar, low in fiber, and lacking in all essential micronutrients. We are among the world leaders in degenerative disease. While we do not have an abundance of poverty ("fill of poverty"), as do so very many of the people throughout the world, we are a people experiencing poverty in the midst of plenty.

Most people in America today have never eaten real bread, the Staff of Life, made from freshly milled flour and filled with all of the fiber and vital nutrients that are present in the wheat berries or other kernels of grain. In this country, we do not have plenty of real bread. We do not have plenty of safe and nutrient-dense grains, beans, fruits, and vegetables. We have pursued vain things. We lack sense. We are indeed impoverished in spite of our affluence.

As an evangelical Christian, the issue of the environment is of great concern to me. I do not support the political agenda going forth in the name of environmentalism. However, I am an environmentalist. *The Oxford Dictionary and Thesaurus* defines an environmentalist as a person who is concerned with or who advocates the protection of the environment.[4] "Environmentalist" is, and will remain, a perfectly good word if we refuse to accept the politicized definition of it. All true Christians and Jews—to name two groups with whom I am most deeply involved—are clearly called to be environmentalists. We are stewards of all that He has given us to use and enjoy. How can we abuse, destroy, or neglect the world that our Father made for us?

In the beginning God created the heavens and the earth.
Genesis 1:1

Then God said, "I give you every seed-bearing plant on
the face of the whole earth and every tree that has
fruit with seed in it. They will be yours for food. And
to all the beasts of the earth and all the birds of the
air and all the creatures that move on the ground—
everything that has the breath of life in it—I give
every green plant for food." And it was so. God saw
all that he had made, and it was very good.

Genesis 1:29-31a

The Message

Learning to Heed the Symptoms of Degeneration (Physical Pain and Discomfort) as Warning Signals

These signals call for our attention. As we mature spiritu-
ally, intellectually, and emotionally, we are better able to understand the signals that our bodies send. On an elementary
level, we do this at very young ages; if we are bleeding, we seek
ways to get the bleeding stopped and to keep the wound clean.
However, if we grow up learning to treat headaches with pain-
killing drugs, indigestion with antacids, and constipation with
laxatives, we are, in effect, learning to shut off the warning
signals without discovering the reasons for our physical problems.

My own interest in learning how to feel better and stron-
ger developed after undergraduate school. During undergraduate school, I paid little attention to my health and physical
well-being. My focus throughout my teens and early twenties
was on the big WHYS—why God, why religion, why the
various political and economic systems. And, of course, I asked
the ultimate question: why are we alive? It is easy to overlook
the significance of learning to stay alive and well when one
hasn't answered the big WHYS.

During undergraduate school I considered agnosticism and
naturalism a reasonable response to the religious faith and
practice I had experienced as an adolescent; and I embraced
Marxist socialism as an answer to the political and economic
questions of the sixties. Then, in my early twenties, I began to
apprehend my own mortality. I struggled with the significance

of time and eternity. As I grappled with the certainty that everything I held dear would eventually pass away, I began seeking a connection between the body, mind, and spirit. I turned to a mixed bag of mysticism and spiritualism and embraced what is commonly called New Age thinking.

In 1969 I walked into a health food store for the first time. That event marked the beginning of my journey as a health researcher. The variety of foods and appliances and the wealth of information that I gathered that afternoon awakened me to the carelessness of my life. Coffee, tea, cigarettes, books, theatre, and people had been the basis of what seemed to me a most enjoyable and stimulating life. The two to three days that I spent each month in bed, dependent upon heavy doses of Darvon and two heating pads, seemed to me to be perfectly normal. Some women suffered menstrual cramps, I figured, and some didn't. I didn't stop to consider why.

Food had never been particularly interesting to me. However, when I began to understand that real food is essential to walking in health and fitness and that the food I chose to eat had a direct bearing on the excruciating pain that I endured each month, I abandoned coffee, cigarettes, and sugar. I eliminated what I understood to be processed and devitalized food. And, although I walked in spiritual darkness during those days, I did come to recognize the connection between dietary and lifestyle habits and disease. Discovering the power of food to heal and to energize made me glad and hopeful.

That awakening occurred nearly thirty years ago. I recognized, at the age of twenty-two, the foolishness of using over-the-counter and prescription drugs merely to relieve symptoms. I sensed that walking in knowledge and discipline would change the course of my life. I knew that I needed to actively seek the wisdom of those who knew something about revitalizing and rebuilding the body.

I had both the enthusiasm and the discipline to pursue the information that interested me. But I lacked vital knowledge concerning optimal health and fitness. What I didn't know could have killed me. I became a vegetarian without having had the wisdom of the centuries passed down to me. I did not eat intact grains and legumes. Instead I followed a regimen of freshly extracted vegetable juice concentrates, raw whole foods (fruits and vegetables), and lots of honey and almonds. I ate far too many servings of fruit. With a genetic predisposition to diabetes, I became severely hypoglycemic within a year (a malady that continued to plague me for nearly two decades). In *Health Begins in Him* (Huntington House Publishers, 1995), I talk about my journey. I embraced a sequence of health regimens, each in a rather thorough way, in an attempt to walk in wellness. Most of the bad advice is still around, and readers often tell us that that portion of the book has shortened their own learning curve.

That was 1970, and I was twenty-three. At that time the government schools still promoted the United States Department of Agriculture food guidelines as though they were based on research and genuine science. Encyclopedias and school textbooks outlined the benefits of the basic four food groups (meat, milk, vegetables/fruits, breads/cereals). I knew nothing about the simplicity, sufficiency, and balance in the dietary regimens followed by the healthiest people in the world. I had never stopped to consider who the healthiest people in the world might be. And the largest and most significant epidemiological study of the century, which firmly established the connection between dietary habits and degenerative disease, was not published until two decades later in 1990.[5] Two thoughts directed my inquiry: (1) I believed that I could get well and grow strong, and (2) I considered it my responsibility to discover how to do that. Although I suffered from hypoglycemia, I learned how to manage the problem by eating whole foods and small meals. Still, I could not miss meals.

Those were the early 1970s, almost a decade before John R. Lee began working with transdermal progesterone cream in his practice. Virtually no one promoted the use of natural progesterone as an important factor in stabilizing blood sugar. That was a decade before what Dr. Lee calls the Revolution even began. That revolution is now being carried out by a grassroots network, which is spreading information about safe and effective ways to overcome hormonal imbalance. The challenge now is to help people understand the real causes of this virtual epidemic of diseases and disorders of the endocrine system. Knowing the cause is the first step to understanding the cure. Although I still maintain a meticulous dietary regimen, I am no longer in danger of a hypoglycemic episode should I miss a meal. Now that I am taking 25 mg of micronized transdermal progesterone cream twice daily, I am able to fast whenever I choose.

In my book *Health Begins in Him, Biblical Steps to Optimal Health and Nutrition*, I discuss the journey that led me to wellness. Research indicates that how we choose to think is one of the main determinants of health. People who truly practice their faith and who trust in the power of prayer, experience on a regular basis the healing flow of endorphins throughout their bodies. When I became interested in health and nutrition in 1969, I certainly had no inkling of that reality. When I first came to Christ in 1974, I did not understand the powerful connection between my thoughts and my physical well-being. But, thank God, we are refined in the press of life; and we learn by the power of the Spirit not to resent and resist adversity but rather to embrace it according to the fifth chapter of Romans.

My first husband, Frank Bunetta, survived a massive heart attack in 1972. Both of us became Christians in 1974. We pursued natural therapies and found information concerning vitamin E therapy, but we had none of the information concerning the prevention and cure of heart disease through dietary and lifestyle change that is now widely available. Frank died of a massive heart attack in March 1978.

Twenty months later, in November 1979, I married Gary Dorian. After two years of marriage and months of testing, physicians diagnosed both Gary and me as infertile. Finally, in the summer of 1982, we asked the elders of the church to anoint us with oil and to pray that I would conceive a child. By the end of the month, I became pregnant with our first child, Jessica. Gary was forty-one years old, and I was thirty-five. Jessica was born in April 1983. Sixteen months later I gave birth to our second child, a daughter, Canaan.

Our third child, Christian, was born in April 1987. That fall my father was diagnosed with non-Hodgkin's lymphoma. Our fourth child, Jenna, was born in August 1988. When my father died in June 1989, I simply failed to acknowledge the depth of my loss or to confess my agony and grief to the One who heals our hearts and binds our wounds. I believe that my response to adversity caused me to degenerate physically.

Dad came to Christ at St. Mary's Hospital in Rochester, Minnesota, in the fall of 1987, soon after the physicians diagnosed his condition. Dad and I prayed together nearly every day during his two-year struggle with cancer. Through his illness and his relationship with the Lord, Dad and I developed a wonderful friendship. He had always been a devoted father and grandfather, but by the power of the Spirit, we became intimate friends. Dad suffered great pain at the end of his struggle with cancer. Through death, the Lord released him from the physical torment of the therapies and of the illness itself. Our great comfort was, and is, the certainty that he is safe and secure in Christ.

In the face of Dad's triumph, I counted my grief as a lack of trust in God and evidence of ingratitude. I was wrong. Scripture teaches us that there is a time to weep and a time to mourn. When we offer our helplessness to Him in trust and adoration, He is our strength, the balm of Gilead. When we ask for grace, He becomes our comfort, our peace. His love is our reality.

In the two years following Dad's death, I continued to deny my emotional pain and spiritual need, and I continued to suffer physically. My dietary habits and lifestyle had remained the same as they had been throughout the years of childbearing and lactating. Those times of pregnancy and lactating marked the healthiest years of my life until the illness and death of my father. Although I had lost the weight I had gained during my pregnancy with Jenna, our fourth child, I began gaining weight a year after Dad's death. By the next year, I was sixty pounds overweight, even though I had made no significant changes in my dietary habits and lifestyle. The hypoglycemia that I had experienced throughout my twenties and thirties—before the years of pregnancy and lactating—returned. Suddenly, I had a full-blown health crisis. I did not know what to do. I had never heard of natural hormones, transdermal progesterone cream, or estrogen dominance. I was not menopausal. I felt terrible.

When I explained my dietary regime (optimal by conventional medical standards) to the gynecologist, he suggested that I keep a food diary. "Why?" I asked, not quite getting it. "Then you'll be able to see what you're really eating." I remained silent. I felt rage. I couldn't function. I looked at my symptoms—sudden weight gain, dizziness and shakiness (relieved by food), unstable blood sugar (in spite of regular meals of whole grains and vegetables), systemic candidiasis, extreme fatigue after meals, and pharyngeal spasms. In spite of my best efforts, and handfuls of nutritional supplements, I continued to degenerate physically. The story of my rapid degeneration and my subsequent recovery and regeneration, is found in *Health Begins in Him.*

Then, I prayed. And in my desperation, I encountered my need. I acknowledged my total dependence on the Lord, and I asked my heavenly Father to tell me how to get well. At the time, I was researching and writing a guide to better eating for a company that manufactures flour mills for use in the home and distributes them worldwide. Suddenly, I realized that if I continued to degenerate, I would not be able to care for myself. Prayer is an incredible privilege that we have as believers. The very act of praying changes our lives. I found unforgiveness in my heart, and I asked for the grace to forgive. Through prayer, I came to realize that fear had overshadowed the words of faith that I so often professed. I asked the Lord to flood my soul with faith, to purify my heart, and to renew my mind.

I walked back through my life in Him to the very moment when the Holy Spirit of God filled me with the revelation of Jesus Christ as my Lord. I remembered with awe what it means to be forgiven, accepted, and clothed in the righteousness of Christ. Then, with a clear mind and thankful heart, I asked the Lord to lead and direct my study. And study I did, trusting Him to give me wisdom and understanding. I would not offer any advice on health and healing without acknowledging the Lord as my source of wisdom and strength in all things.

As I proclaim my faith in Him, I must express my thankfulness for the people from many faiths, and the people with no faith, whose insight, research, expertise, and integrity have blessed my life. No, I do not think that all roads lead to eternal truth. I believe in the inerrancy of the Word of God and trust in the words of the Lord Jesus Christ when He says, "I am the way and the truth and the life. No one comes to the Father except through me." (John 14:6) But, as I seek wisdom and knowledge in the routine business of living, I trust that by His Word and through the power of His Spirit, I will be able to recognize and celebrate wisdom and justice, wherever I find it. Individuals, institutions, and organizations need affirmation when their deeds are worthy of our praise.

Although I left the New Age movement over twenty-five years ago, I have not forgotten the many friends and counselors along the way. Those who remain in touch with me know that I no longer identify with "Mother Earth" or attribute the mastery of the universe to the forces of "Nature." And, yet, we enjoy the blessing of working together on common goals. I am so very grateful for the opportunity to share research and information with a diverse group of colleagues. We are of different races and from different ethnic groups. We define and express our faith in many ways. I believe we recognize this diversity as an answer to our prayers for compassion, insight, and understanding. Embracing diversity encourages us to face that which is incomprehensible to us with the love of God, the mind of Christ, and the gentleness of the Spirit. With an inquiring mind and a humble spirit, we recognize the necessity of an interdisciplinary approach to health and fitness that grows out of an appreciation for the liberal arts and education, as well as science and technology. Biblical studies, ancient history, cultural anthropology, food science, nutritional science, exercise physiology, medical science, biochemistry, epidemiology, and many other academic disciplines allow us to fully explore what constitutes an optimal diet and lifestyle.

In part one I address what I call the Madness in order that people might avoid deception and walk in wisdom and abundant life. I also address the message we receive from physical pain and symptoms. When our bodies send a signal of alarm, we need to ask why. The symptoms of perimenopause, menopause, postmenopause, premenopause, and andropause awaken us to first seek the causes of our problems. Only then can we find solutions. Those who are suffering from hormonal imbalance need to know what is going wrong in their bodies and then learn how to correct the problems. This book will enable readers to understand, according to the research, the reasons for hormonal imbalance. Readers will also discover, according to the research, how to find safe and efficacious solutions for the problem of hormonal imbalance. I trust that these are worthy goals: to seek health and healing for ourselves, for our families and friends, and for a hurting world; to discern, by His grace, what is right and what is wrong; to distinguish facts from fallacies; to walk in wisdom, and to abandon foolishness.

> Don't worry about the wicked.
> Don't envy those who do wrong.
> For like grass, they soon fade away.
> Like springtime flowers, they soon wither.
>
> Trust in the LORD and do good.
> Then you will live safely in the land and prosper.
> Take delight in the LORD,
> and he will give you your heart's desires. . . .
>
> I myself have seen it happen—
> proud and evil people thriving like mighty trees.
> But when I looked again, they were gone!
> Though I searched for them, I could not find them!
> Psalm 37:1-4, 35-36 (NLT)

Notes

1. Lee, John R., M.D., *Natural Progesterone: The Multiple Roles of a Remarkable Hormone.* Revised ed. (Sebastopol, CA: BLL Publishing, 1993, 1997), 88.

2. Robert Pear, "Tougher Labeling for Organic Food," *New York Times,* 9 May 1998, A1.

3. Chen J., T.C. Campbell, Li J., R. Peto, *Diet, Lifestyle, and Mortality in China: A Study of the Characteristics of Sixty-Five Chinese Counties* (Oxford, UK: Oxford University Press; Ithaca, NY: Cornell University Press; Beijing, PRC: People's Medical Publishing House, 1990).

4. *Oxford Dictionary and Thesaurus,* American ed. (New York: Oxford University Press, 1966), s.v. "environmentalist."

5. Chen, et al., *Diet, Lifestyle, and Mortality in China.*

The Big Lie

Those who are suffering from hormonal imbalance, or who are concerned about those who are suffering, want answers to these basic and urgent questions:

1. Do scientists know the causes of hormonal imbalance?

2. Are there safe and effective ways to achieve hormonal balance during every life cycle (i.e., the childbearing years, perimenopause, menopause, and postmenopause)?

3. If there are safe and effective solutions to hormonal imbalance, why does the medical community support therapies such as ERT (estrogen replacement therapy) and HRT (hormone replacement therapy)? Both therapies are either (a) somewhat effective, but clearly unsafe and life threatening (if we're to believe the information on the manufacturer's package insert) or (b) clearly ineffective and also unsafe and life threatening.

> Author's note for those who do not fully understand the life stages of the female: The childbearing years begin at menarche and continue until significant changes occur in hormone secretions. The perimenopausal period begins with the onset of significant changes in hormone secretions and continues until menstrual periods cease. The menopausal period begins when menstrual periods cease; however, the onset of menopause is actually defined as the time when a woman has missed twelve

consecutive menstrual periods. The postmenopausal
period is the time of life after menstruation has ceased
(whether the cessation of menstruation has occurred
naturally or as the result of surgery).

Before we present the clear, research-based answers to
questions one and two, we need to answer the big WHY of
question three. There is an art and a science to walking in
wellness. On our way to recognizing the truth in science, many
of us learn to become seekers of truth through the humanities.
Part Two answers question three. Part Three answers both
question one and question two.

The Emperor's New Clothes, a tale created by master story-
teller Hans Christian Andersen, illustrates the ways in which
human pride can turn us into co-conspirators, who are willing
to deny reality and participate in deception. If we carefully
examine the thoughts and behaviors of the characters in Hans
Christian Andersen's story, we will find that the Emperor's
complete lack of interest in the needs of his kingdom is analo-
gous to the medical industrial establishment's failure to support true science, health, and healing. After each segment of
Hans Christian Andersen's story, I share a segment from my
takeoff, *The Monarch's New Medicine.* I hope that my version
of Andersen's story, together with my story—presented simul-
taneously—will accomplish the following: (1) clarify the present
deception concerning ERT and HRT, and (2) aptly characterize the actions of those who continue to endorse ERT and
HRT as reasonable choices. Perhaps this exercise will challenge us to resist being distracted by those who present a false
dilemma concerning ERT and HRT and challenge us to focus
on promoting the real issues concerning hormonal balance.

The   Emperor's   New   Clothes

by   Hans   Christian   Andersen
retold   by   Terry   Dorian,   Ph.D.

*Long ago an Emperor lived in a great land. He spent
all his time and all his money on clothes in order to
be extraordinarily well dressed. He did not show*

concern for his soldiers, nor did he go to the theatre, nor did he ride about his kingdom—except to show off his beautiful new clothes. He paraded about in a dazzling new garment every hour of the day.

The Monarch's New Medicine

by Terry Dorian, Ph.D.

Long ago, in the second half of the twentieth century, a Medical Monarch set himself up as the supreme advisor on the health and welfare of everyone in the land. He had such an interest in the development of new and patentable medicines that he spent nearly all his time looking at new formulas and research studies supporting their use. He did not consider ways to actually remedy the health crises of the people; rather, he imagined medicines that the Pharmaceutical Princes could develop to treat the symptoms of disease. He thought of every disease in terms of profit.

The people of the kingdom asked, "What is the Emperor doing?" Instead of answering, "He is talking to his Ministers," his officers answered, "The Emperor is in his dressing room, deciding what to wear." The people in the Emperor's big town passed the time merrily. A variety of visitors arrived every day at court. One day two men who called themselves weavers came to court. The men really made their living robbing other people by telling them such fantastic lies that the people thought the lies were true.

The people of the kingdom asked, "What is the Medical Monarch doing?" Instead of answering, "The Monarch is talking to the heads of the major medical schools in the land. He is encouraging them to study ways to prevent and cure degenerative disease with non-toxic therapies and probiotic formulations," his attendants would reply, "The Monarch is reviewing the latest patents and counting the profits from the old ones." The people in the Monarch's land passed the time merrily. Many of them had plenty of money to spend. They followed the Medical Monarch's Dietary Guidelines, which supported the meat and dairy interests. Most people enjoyed hearty meals of meat and dairy (laden with hormones and pesticide residues), together with sugar and processed, devitalized grain products—all of which appeared on the Medical Monarch's Department of Agriculture Food Guide Pyramid. Then, the Medical Monarch sold them his patent medicines for all their maladies.

A variety of visitors arrived at court. One day two men, who said they had special gifts and abilities in scientific research, came to court. The men really made their living in the pharmaceutical industry making such fantastic claims that the people thought the claims must be true, and the costly products must be superior. These two men, who were unusually deceitful Pharmaceutical Princes, came to call on the Medical Monarch.[1]

> The men talked about their skill in weaving cloth with extraordinary colors and patterns. They convinced everyone who heard them speak that the clothes made from this magic cloth could not be seen by anyone who was unfit for the position he held or who lacked intelligence. The only people who could see these beautiful clothes were those who were truly fit for the positions they held and who were highly intelligent.

The unusually deceitful Pharmaceutical Princes talked about the scientific training and technological expertise that enabled them to make hormones with molecular structures different from (and superior to) the molecular structures of the hormones made by the human body. Moreover, they said, "The superiority of the formulations (in the case of conjugated estrogens like Premarin) or the altered molecular structure (in the case of ethinyl estradiol, a synthetic estrogen) cannot be understood by anyone who is unfit to be a medical doctor or who lacks intelligence. Two of these extraordinary formulations, Premarin and Provera, and a variety of synthetic estrogens and progestins, are only recognized as medical breakthroughs by those who are fit to be medical doctors or who are highly intelligent."

"These must be incredible clothes," thought the Emperor. "If the weavers make me a suit out of this magic cloth, I will be able to determine which men in my kingdom are fit for the positions they hold and which men are not. I will be able to know who is wise and who is foolish. I must direct them to begin weaving the cloth immediately." And he ordered the Treasurer to give large sums of money to the two weavers in order that they might begin their work at once.

"These must be incredible hormones!" thought the Medical Monarch. "If I begin recommending these hormones to all the medical doctors and to all the women in the country, I will find out at once which medical doctors in my kingdom are not fit to practice medicine. I will be able to know who is wise and who is foolish. I must direct them to begin producing these hormones immediately and to begin designing research studies to support their safety and efficacy." He then ordered the Treasurer to give large sums of money to the Pharmaceutical Princes in order that they might begin their work at once.

So the two men who called themselves weavers set up two looms and went through all the motions of working on the great looms, though in reality the looms had no thread on them at all. They asked for precious silk and costly gold thread. They kept these materials for themselves, hid them away in their knapsacks, and continued to move their bodies as though they were actually working the great looms. They did their pretended work at the empty looms late into the night.

So the two men, who said they had special scientific training and technological experience, busied themselves. They reviewed the unique ways in which they had developed the synthetic compounds by adding atoms at unusual positions to the molecular structure of natural hormones. They continued to design studies supporting the safety and efficacy of both their synthetic compounds and their conjugated estrogens. "Of course," they insisted, "they are an improvement over the hormones produced by the human body. The formula

(Premarin) made from equilin and equilenin (horse estrogens), and which also contains huge amounts of estrone, shows particular genius!"

They ignored the research indicating that such large amounts of estrone could cause cancer. They continued to refer to their work as "true science" and to number the ways women could benefit from the extraordinary hormone formulations. They designed more studies involving medical doctors at major universities and funded the studies. The studies seemed difficult and authoritative to most of the people in the land, so difficult and authoritative that many people imagined them to be scholarly. This made the deceptive Pharmaceutical Princes seem honorable. Then, the media helped them to celebrate the outcome of the research studies. Women in the land thought that all of this had something to do with improving the quality of their lives—a way of living better and longer through chemistry. The Pharmaceutical Princes continued planning advertising campaigns far into the night. When they finished, they counted all the money that they would make on their patented formulas.

After awhile the Emperor thought to himself, "I would like to know how well the weavers are doing with my cloth. I am slightly hesitant about going myself to look at the cloth because they said that a person who lacks intelligence or who is unfit for his position is unable to see the material. I am sure that I would have no trouble seeing the material, but all the same I think it would be wise for me to send someone else first."

After awhile the Medical Monarch said to himself, "I would like to know how the Pharmaceutical Princes are doing with the extraordinary hormones that are superior to the molecular structure of those hormones that are made by the human body. I am a little bit worried about asking the Pharmaceutical Princes how these conjugated estrogens and synthetic compounds could possibly be better than those hormones made by the body. They said that these formulas could not be understood by anyone who is unfit to be a medical doctor or who lacks intelligence. I am sure that I could easily understand the research studies and genius behind these formulations. Nevertheless, I think it would be best to send a highly esteemed medical doctor to discuss the formulations first.

The people in the Emperor's town and throughout the land had already heard about the extraordinary cloth and its magic. The people wanted to know how wise or how stupid their friends and neighbors might be.

The people in the Medical Monarch's city and across the land had already heard of the extraordinary hormones. They were anxious to know who could understand the significance of the studies and the genius behind the formulations. Then, they would know how wise or how stupid their friends and neighbors might be. They would also find out whether or not their medical doctors were fit to practice medicine.

"I will send my faithful old Minister to see how the weavers are getting on with my cloth," said the Emperor after a great deal of thought. "He is the best possible person to grasp the wonder of the cloth for he is truly fit for his position and he is without question a person of high intelligence."

Finally, the Medical Monarch reached a decision: "I will send my friend and mentor the honest old Medical Doctor. He is on more boards and has more impressive credentials than anyone in the country. He will understand why these formulas are beneficial. He is a man of sense and no one could be more fit to be a medical doctor than he."

The honest old Minister found the wicked men going through all the physical motions of working at the looms. "What is the meaning of this?" thought the old man, with eyes wide open and fixed on the empty looms. "I cannot see any thread on these looms nor can I see any cloth woven!" However, he did not dare tell these men who called themselves weavers what he was thinking.

The honest old Medical Doctor (who was a consultant in Obstetrics and Gynecology for many of the major teaching hospitals in the kingdom) found the unusually deceptive Pharmaceutical Princes poring over the research studies supporting the safety and efficacy of their extraordinary hormones. As the men explained the ways in which the molecular structures had been altered by the addition of atoms, he thought to himself, "What is the meaning of this?" As the honest old Medical Doctor thought more and more about their extraordinary hormones, he opened his eyes wide. He said to himself, "I cannot see any way these hormones could be more beneficial to women than the hormones with the same molecular structure as those made by the human body." He remembered the words of a dedicated physician, who had years of experience with bio-identical hormones. The true science of his colleague's words came to mind: "These synthetic steroids are not subject to the usual metabolic control provided by our enzymes; their effects cannot be tuned down or turned off, and moreover, these synthetic compounds cannot be efficiently excreted by the body's usual enzymatic mechanisms."[2] However, he did not quote his colleague's words aloud.

> As the men continued to go through the motions of weaving, they turned to the honest old Minister. They asked him, in very polite tones, if he would please examine the cloth very closely and say whether or not he liked the design and whether or not he agreed that the colors were indeed quite spectacular.

The deceitful Pharmaceutical Princes continued to talk as though they had been conducting scientific research and doing scholarly studies. They asked the honest old Medical Doctor if he would closely examine their studies and be so good as to share his insight with them. The Pharmaceutical Princes boasted of their creativity for having revitalized the female body with the urine of pregnant mares and asked the old Medical Doctor whether he was pleased with the amazing benefits of the conjugated estrogens they called Premarin. They also began lecturing him on the benefits of their synthetic estrogens and progestin.

The poor old Minister stared and stared at the looms with the hope that the cloth would be visible to him, but he could not see anything on the looms. The reason the cloth did not become visible to him was that there was, in fact, no cloth there! But, of course, he could not know this and thought only that he must be a foolish man or unfit for the office of Minister. "Dear me," he said to himself, "I must never tell anyone that the extraordinary cloth is not visible to me."

The poor old Medical Doctor thought and thought about the conclusions of the Pharmaceutical Princes and strained to imagine how in the world conjugated estrogens, which contain equilin and equilenin (horse estrogens), could possibly be safe, even though they could relieve some of the symptoms of hormonal imbalance. But, in the face of all evidence to the contrary, he could not imagine it. So, he thought he must be very foolish and unfit to be a medical doctor. "Dear me," he said to himself, "I must never tell anyone that I could not see the benefit in giving women horse estrogens, or synthetic estrogens and progestins."

"Well, Sir Minister," said one of the weavers, still going through the physical motions of weaving at the looms, "You have not told us whether or not our cloth pleases you!" "Oh! It is most extraordinary!" said the Minister. He then quickly peered at the loom through his spectacles. "This pattern and the colors are like no others I have seen! Yes, I will go to the Emperor immediately and tell him that this cloth is everything that he could wish."

"Well, dear Doctor," said one of the unusually deceitful Pharmaceutical Princes, trying to appear engrossed in study, "You have not told us what you think about our conjugated estrogens, synthetic estrogens, and progestins." "Oh!" said the honest old Medical Doctor, "The impact the horse estrogens, and the synthetic estrogens and progestins could make on the lives of hundreds of thousands of women is truly unimaginable!" Then he quickly added, "What vision and

genius! Yes, I will tell the Medical Monarch without delay
these hormones are everything that he could wish, and they
will impact the lives of millions of women."

*"We are most grateful for your insight and abili-
ties," said the men who pretended to be weavers,
and they began to describe the cloth in detail. The
old Minister listened closely to their impressive
words so that he could accurately describe the cloth
to the Emperor. Then the wicked men requested
more silk and gold in order to finish what they had
begun. Again the Emperor gave them the costly
thread and silk, and again they put all of it into their
knapsacks and continued to go through the physical
motions of working at the looms as busily as before.*

"We are most grateful for your insight and abilities," said
the Pharmaceutical Princes, and they began to discuss the
outstanding points in each study in great detail. The old
doctor listened closely as they discussed the cross-sectional
studies, prospective studies, cohort studies, case controlled
studies, and randomized controlled clinical trials. The doctor
listened to their impressive findings so that he could repeat
them to the Medical Monarch. Then, the wicked men requested more money from the Medical Monarch to do more
studies on the extraordinary hormones. They needed more
studies in order to convince the people in the land that these
hormones are indeed superior to those hormones that are
identical to those made by the human body. Again, the Medical Monarch gave them more money. The Pharmaceutical
Princes used it to fund the studies that would support the
safety and efficacy of their products.

*The Emperor patted the Minister on the back when
he heard his report and soon after sent another
officer of his court to evaluate the work of the
weavers and to determine how soon the cloth would
be ready.*

The Medical Monarch patted the old Medical Doctor on
the back when he heard his report; and soon after sent

another representative from his kingdom to evaluate the work of the Pharmaceutical Princes and to determine how soon the studies could be released to the general public. The worker, who held a regulatory job with the FDA (Food and Drug Administration), was qualified (according to his job description) to investigate products and research. The FDA worker went to the unusually deceitful Pharmaceutical Princes to examine their research studies and to determine whether or not their extraordinary hormones were both safe and efficacious. He really wanted to find out how they compared to the hormones manufactured by the human body! But the Pharmaceutical Princes said, "We are certainly not going to waste our time, or the Medical Monarch's money, in order to investigate bio-identical hormones that can't be patented, and no one else is going to either. No one is interested in bio-identical hormones anyway. Science and technology open up a world of possibilities for those who can understand the remarkable achievements that have been made. We have developed extraordinarily effective hormones superior to anything made by the human body."

> *The officer saw the same thing on the looms as the Minister had seen—nothing. He stared at the looms wishing that the cloth would appear before his eyes, but he saw nothing at all. "Do you think the cloth is as extraordinary as the Minister thinks it is?" asked the men, as they gestured toward the empty looms and talked of the design and colors of the cloth that was not there.*

The worker had the same difficulties with the studies and the hormones that the old Medical Doctor had—he could not understand why in the world anyone would want to use synthetic compounds or horse estrogens instead of bio-identical hormones.

The worker strained and strained to imagine how in the world equilin and equilenin could possibly be safe, even though they could help relieve some of the symptoms of hormonal imbalance. He examined the research data on the synthetic estrogens and progestins, and he wondered why anyone would want to take these synthetic compounds rather than the hormones that are identical to those made by the human body—if they realized that they had a choice.

Then, the unusually deceitful Pharmaceutical Princes pointed to their voluminous research studies and congratulated each other on the creative genius of using horse urine and synthetic compounds to enable women to overcome the debilitating symptoms of menopause, and to prevent heart disease, memory loss, and osteoporosis. The Pharmaceutical Princes then turned to the worker from the FDA and asked, "Are you as confident of the impact our extraordinary hormones will make on the lives of millions of women as was the Medical Doctor sent by the Medical Monarch?"

"I know that I do not lack intelligence," thought the officer. "I must not be fit for the very good comfortable office I have. That is very disturbing. However, I'm not going to let anyone know what I'm thinking." And at once he turned to the men who called themselves weavers and praised the material he could not see, saying that he was delighted with both the colors and the patterns.

"I know that I do not lack intelligence," thought the worker, who was very pleased with the regulatory job he held with the FDA. Then, he took a deep breath and came to some sobering conclusions: "I must not be fit for the task of properly evaluating such highly technical scientific data. I clearly have no training or expertise in this area of inquiry, because I cannot understand why these hormones represent such a remarkable achievement. However, no one shall ever know anything about my lack of qualifications." And at once he turned to the unprincipled, profit-oriented Pharmaceutical Princes, and praised them for the contributions they were making to the advancement of science.

When the officer returned to the Emperor he said, "Indeed, Your Imperial Majesty, the cloth that the weavers are making is extraordinarily magnificent."

When the worker returned to the Medical Monarch, he said, "Indeed, Your Royal Majesty, the hormones that the Royal Highnesses, the Pharmaceutical Princes, are making are extraordinarily advanced scientifically."

People throughout the land talked about the incredible cloth that the Emperor had ordered to be woven at such great expense.

People throughout the kingdom talked about the incredible hormones, superior to any that the body could produce, that the Medical Monarch had ordered to be developed and studied at such a great cost. What most of the people in the land did not know was that the Medical Monarch and the pharmaceutical industry spent hundreds of millions of dollars in the development of each new drug. Most of the people also did not know that part of those hundreds of millions were allocated for regulatory jobs at the FDA (Food and Drug Administration) and another part of those hundreds of millions were spent on huge promotional allowances for the nation's 479,000 doctors. The information was available, of course, buried in a GAO (General Accounting Office) report in Washington, D.C.[3]

Most of the people in the land had been too busy either to read the exposé in Time magazine, or to think much about what they might do to voice their protest. The exposé detailed the benefits that medical doctors received from the Pharmaceutical Princes (i.e., the pharmaceutical industry). Wyeth-Ayerst Laboratories gave "doctors each 1,000 points on American Airlines' frequent-flyer program for each patient they put on the hypertension drug Inderal LA," and Ciba-Geigy offered free Caribbean vacations to doctors for attending lectures about Estraderm, an estrogen patch.[4]

Finally, the Emperor decided to go himself and see the marvelous cloth while it was still on the loom. He chose a few officers of the court to go with him. And, of course, he wanted the Minister and the officer who had already seen the cloth to go back again and share his excitement.

Finally, the Medical Monarch decided to go himself and review the scientific data supporting the safety and efficacy of the extraordinary formulations—Premarin, Provera, and a variety of synthetic estrogens and progestins. He took with him a few of the physicians from the country's top medical schools. He took the two men (his honest old Medical Doctor, who was a consultant in Obstetrics and Gynecology, and the worker who held a regulatory job with the FDA) who had reviewed the scientific studies. He wanted them to go back again and share his excitement over the extraordinary impact the hormones would make on the women in the land.

When the weavers heard the Emperor coming, they quickly began going through the physical motions of weaving thread through the looms. Of course, they did not weave a single thread through the empty looms.

When the unprincipled, profit-conscious Pharmaceutical Princes heard that the Medical Monarch was coming, they busied themselves preparing press releases for both the print and electronic media. They outlined the significant points in each study that they wished to have highlighted by the most esteemed men and women in the medical community. Then, they began to think of incentives for the medical doctors in the land. "We could do what Roche did," one of them said. "Great!" the other answered, "Remember when they paid doctors $1200 if they prescribed the antibiotic Rocephin for twenty hospital patients? That made the doctors part of their 'study.' "[5] They grinned.

"Isn't this cloth remarkable?" asked the officer and the Minister who had already discovered that the cloth was not visible to them. "Just look at the cloth, Your Majesty. Have you ever seen such brilliant colors or such extraordinary design?" They pointed to the empty frames as they described the cloth that they could not see. They thought for certain that everyone else could see the wonderful cloth, even though they could not see it themselves.

"*Aren't these studies remarkable?*" asked the worker and the honest old Medical Doctor. "*Do these studies not prove that the formulations developed by the Pharmaceutical Princes are, indeed, extraordinary?*" they also asked. "*Would Your Royal Majesty be so good as to consider the level of training and expertise behind these cross-sectional, prospective, cohort, and case controlled studies together with the randomized controlled clinical trials?*" urged the old Medical Doctor. They pointed to the expertise and training behind the studies, because they thought for certain that everyone else could see how the horse estrogens and the synthetic compounds were an improvement over the hormones that were identical to those produced by the human body. They thought everyone else could understand why these hormones represented a remarkable scientific achievement, even though they could not understand it themselves.

"What is this?" the Emperor asked himself, "I don't see anything on the looms! This is frightening! Am I a foolish man or am I unfit to be Emperor? I must decide how to handle this very difficult situation!"

"*What is this?*" the Medical Monarch asked himself, "*I don't see any benefits in using these conjugated estrogens that contain equilin and equillenin. And, I do not see why any woman would choose to take conjugated estrogens or synthetic estrogens and progestins. Who would want to risk the known side effects with these products when safe, bio-identical hormones are available? This is frightening! Am I a foolish man or am I unfit to be the Medical Monarch? I must decide how to handle this very difficult situation.*"

"Oh, the cloth is extraordinary!" he exclaimed. "I am so very delighted with it," he said, smiling gratefully. He purposed to make certain that no one would detect that the very cloth that his officer and Minister had found so extraordinary was not even visible to him.

"*Oh, the studies are indeed conclusive! These hormones are most extraordinary, and they are clearly superior to those*

made by the human body," he exclaimed. "What an advancement in medical science," he said, smiling gratefully. He
purposed to make certain that no one would detect that he
could not understand why these hormones represented such
a remarkable scientific advancement. After all, the worker
(from the FDA) and his friend, the honest old Medical Doctor,
found the research studies conclusive and compelling!

> Everyone in the Emperor's entourage stared at the
> looms, hoping to see the cloth, not realizing that no
> one could see the cloth because there was no cloth
> to see! Nevertheless, everyone exclaimed, "Oh,
> how beautiful!" And they advised His Majesty the
> Emperor to get new clothes made from this extraor-
> dinary material and wear them in the great proces-
> sion that was about to take place.

Everyone in the Medical Monarch's entourage considered it a privilege to be in the company of the heads of the
Departments of Obstetrics and Gynecology at the major
teaching hospitals in the kingdom. Everyone in the entourage
stared at the research summaries, trying to find something
compelling in the research. But no one could understand
from the studies why the hormones were regarded as extraordinary. Nevertheless, they all exclaimed, "Oh, these new
hormones are indeed extraordinary!" They advised His Majesty, the Medical Monarch, to organize a media campaign,
and announce the important research findings to all the
people in the land, and to hold a televised news conference
in the Palace Rose Garden.

> "Impressive! A work of art!" they said over and
> over again and everyone celebrated the accomplish-
> ments of the weavers. The Emperor acted as though
> he were as happy as the people in his entourage, and
> he granted the two rogues special awards of honor
> and   distinction.

"Impressive! A scientific breakthrough! An end to the
malaise of menopause! A key to the prevention of osteoporosis,
heart disease, and Alzheimer's disease!" they said over and
over again, and everyone celebrated the accomplishments of

the Pharmaceutical Princes. The Medical Monarch acted as though he was as happy as the people in his entourage, and he granted the Pharmaceutical Princes special certificates of merit and awards of service. He pretended to be as impressed and pleased as the men and women who headed the Departments of Obstetrics and Gynecology. At a ceremony, everyone gave special honor to Robert A. Wilson, M.D., as the most distinguished spokesman for the popular estrogen replacement formula, Premarin. The Pharmaceutical Princes had a real salesman in Dr. Robert A. Wilson, a New York gynecologist who wrote Feminine Forever, published in 1966 and underwritten by the Pharmaceutical Princes (the Ayerst laboratories). Dr. Wilson's book promoted the concept of menopause as an estrogen deficiency disease, and he promoted conjugated estrogens containing equilin and equilenin as the cure. A hundred thousand copies of Dr. Wilson's book were sold in seven months. Magazines throughout the land popularized these extraordinary new hormones and established the concept of menopause as a disease.[6]

> The wicked men sat at their looms all night pretending to get ready for the procession that would take place the next day. They kept lights burning all night so that everyone could see how eager they were to finish the Emperor's new clothes. They gestured as though they were rolling the cloth off the looms. Then they cut into the air with their scissors as though they were cutting fabric and sewed with their needles as though they had thread. "At last we have finished!" they exclaimed. "We have finished making the Emperor's new clothes!"

The Pharmaceutical Princes worked months and years, planning better and better ways to capture the attention of the entire female population in the land. They sent out regular press releases in order to popularize Dr. Robert Wilson's new book.

They tried to win more and more physicians over to their concept of menopause as a disease that could be cured with estrogen. If estrogen-deficient women took the extraordinary hormones, they would be cured of menopause! They would

*lower their risk of dying from heart disease and of suffering
from osteoporosis and memory loss!*

*A virtual army of physicians in the land had read Dr.
Wilson's own summary of the main arguments of his book.
He carefully listed the major points in his last chapter, hero-
ically entitled "A Salute to Tomorrow's Woman." The Pharmaceutical Princes demonstrated marketing expertise. Their
media campaign was most successful. Physicians and patients began to think that the research had established all that
the pharmaceutical companies said that it had established.
"See," the Pharmaceutical Princes cried at last, "Our extraordinary hormones, which are superior to the molecular structure of those made by the human body, are ready to be
enthusiastically received by the women in the land!"*

> *The Emperor and all his court hurried to see the
> weavers' work. The rogues pretended to hold up the
> Monarch's trousers, scarf, and coat. "The whole
> suit is as light as a feather!" they exclaimed. They
> laughed to themselves as they held the imaginary
> garments in the air.*

> *"It will seem to Your Majesty that you have noth-
> ing on at all. What a wonder this magic cloth really
> is! Aren't these the most extraordinarily beautiful
> and delicate clothes that you have ever seen?" asked
> the men who pretended to be weavers. "Yes, in-
> deed!" said every member of the Emperor's Court,
> even though they could not see anything at all.*

*And now, the Medical Monarch and all of the many men
and women heading the Departments of Obstetrics and Gynecology came to evaluate the research studies supporting the
safety and efficacy of the extraordinary hormones (conjugated
estrogens containing horse estrogens, and synthetic estrogens and progestins). The Pharmaceutical Princes handed
out pages of quotations from Dr. Robert Wilson's book,* Feminine Forever.[7] *They smiled proudly, as though his words
reflected the best thinking in science and medicine:*

*"The term 'conjugated' refers to the chemical linkage of
compounds occurring naturally in the living body. Prepared*

from the urine of mares in whose bodies this chemical linkage is accomplished, conjugated estrogens are now available in convenient tablet form." (p. 113)

"In more than forty years of gynecological practice, I have administered estrogen to an estimated total of 5,000 women. To the best of my knowledge, my personal work in this area represents by a wide margin the greatest accumulation of clinical data by any single practitioner." (p. 113)

"In the closing of my medical career, I take a perhaps pardonable pride in the fact that the sheer bulk of medical statistics drawn from my work seems to augur a widening acceptance of this vital [estrogen] therapy." (p. 114)

"Estrogen therapy, far from causing cancer, tends to prevent it." (p. 158)

"I have already cited the report in the Journal of the American Medical Association *of 27 October 1962, on a group of 304 women treated with estrogen for periods up to twenty-seven years. According to the norm for non-treated women, eighteen cases of breast or uterine cancer would normally be expected in this group. Yet among the estrogen-treated women, not a single case occurred . . . Why then, in the face of such evidence, does so much mistrust still persist toward a form of therapy that spells promise and hope for every woman alive?" (p. 159)*

"The myth that estrogen is a causative factor in cancer has been proven to be entirely false. On the contrary, indications are that estrogen acts as a cancer preventive. Certainly, the continuance of regular menstruation throughout life has a healthful cleansing effect on uterine tissues and seemingly reduces the incidence of uterine cancer." (p. 207)

"Menopausal symptoms, such as weakening of bones and muscles, dowager's hump, gastro-intestinal disorders, heart trouble, hardening of the arteries, atrophy of the breasts and sexual organs, disturbed vision, wrinkling of the skin, pains in the joints, etc., can be avoided by pre-menopausal therapy and often cured by post-menopausal therapy." (p. 207)

"While progesterone . . . can be regarded as the typical hormone of pregnancy, estrogen may be termed the hormone of feminine attraction and well-being." (p. 62)

"Estrogen therapy doesn't change *a woman. On the contrary:* it keeps her from changing. *Therapy does not alter the natural hormone balance. Rather, it restores the total hormone pattern to the normal, premenopausal level." (p. 53)*

"Yes, indeed!" said all the men and women heading the Departments of Obstetrics and Gynecology at the most prestigious teaching hospitals in the country. However, none of them could see anything in the voluminous studies to support the notion that conjugated estrogens, containing horse estrogens or synthetic estrogens and progestins, were superior to the molecular structure of those hormones made by the human body. Nor did they see any evidence that they were indeed safe.

> *"Please, Your Imperial Majesty, take off your clothes. Allow us to dress you in front of the mirror." After the men who pretended to be weavers undressed the Emperor, they dressed him in his new imaginary, invisible, and totally non-existent clothes! The Emperor turned around and around pretending to admire himself in his new garments.*

"Please, Your Royal Majesty, the Medical Monarch," said the unusually deceitful Pharmaceutical Princes as time went by, "we need your signed remarks urging the physicians in the land to heed the research. We need you to advise the more than forty million American women who will reach menopause by the year 2000 to find a physician who will explain to them the benefits of taking our safe, efficacious, conjugated estrogens." The Medical Monarch then gave his strongest recommendation for the use of what the Pharmaceutical Princes proclaimed to be safe, efficacious, and extraordinary hormones. They pretended to provide him with continual proof of their product's safety and significance. They reminded the Medical Monarch often of the credentials of their spokesman, Dr. Robert Wilson. They recited his degrees, affiliations, and associations:

Consultant in Obstetrics and Gynecology,
Methodist Hospital, Brooklyn, NY

*Consultant in Obstetrics and Gynecology,
St. Mary's Hospital, Brooklyn, NY*

*Consultant in Obstetrics and Gynecology,
Putnam Community Hospital, Carmel, NY*

*Diplomate of the American Board of Obstetrics
and Gynecology*

Diplomate of the International College of Surgeons

Fellow of the American College of Surgeons

Fellow of the International College of Surgeons

*Founder-Fellow of the American College of
Obstetricians and Gynecologists*

Fellow of the American Geriatrics Society

Fellow of the New York Academy of Medicine

Fellow of the New York Gynecological Society

Life-Fellow of the Brooklyn Gynecological Society

*Fellow of the American Medical Association and
the Medical Society of the State of New York*

Member of the American Fertility Society

Member of the American Society of Cytology

Member of the International Fertility Association

Member of the Pan-American Medical Association

Member of the Gerontological Society

Member of the Society for the Advancement of Science

Member of the American Medical Writers Association

*President, The Wilson Research Foundation,
New York, NY[8]*

Although the Medical Monarch continued to feel miserable and inadequate because he could not understand the benefit of the conjugated estrogens and the synthetic compounds, he spoke with authority, clothed, as it were, in Dr.

Robert A. Wilson's credentials. In fact, he rejoiced in the fact that Dr. Wilson's credentials were listed in the back of his authoritative and popular book, Feminine Forever. *The Medical Monarch urged every physician in the land to promote the book, much to the delight of the Pharmaceutical Princes. In his book, Dr. Wilson recommends taking conjugated estrogens in order to be feminine forever and declares that estrogen prevents cancer.[9]*

However, less than a decade from the release of Dr. Robert Wilson's authoritative and popular book came the release of an article in the New England Journal of Medicine *entitled "Increased Risk of Endometrial Carcinoma among Users of Conjugated Estrogens."[10] Being clothed in Dr. Robert A. Wilson's credentials would prove to be no sort of covering at all!*

> *"Your Majesty looks elegant and radiant in his new clothes! They fit perfectly!" everyone cried out. "What an extraordinary design! What beautiful colors! Your robes are truly fit for an Emperor!"*

"Your Majesty is both brilliant and compassionate in his recommendations to the women in the land!" everyone cried out. "What insight! What genius! What magnanimity for having sought out these new medicines, for having ensured proper funding for their research, for having spread knowledge of their extraordinary value to the people in the kingdom! They are indeed hormones superior to the molecular structure of those hormones made by the human body. And indeed, the superiority of these hormones cannot be understood by anyone who is unfit to be a medical doctor or who is very foolish!"

> *"The canopy is waiting, Your Majesty. Your attendants will carry it over you in the procession," explained the minister directing the grand event. "I am ready to begin," declared the Emperor. "How do you think my clothing fits me?" he asked, turning himself around in front of the mirror. He wanted everyone to see that he was absorbed in the magnificence of his wonderful new clothes.*

"The research data and statistics are organized on your great library table and piled on the other desks and tables around the room, Your Majesty," explained the director of Media Relations. "I am ready to begin," declared the Medical Monarch. "Is all of the research concerning the new, lowered dosages of Premarin outlined? Are the Pharmaceutical Princes sure that this answers the issue of safety raised in the New England Journal article? Are all of the men and women heading the Departments of Obstetrics and Gynecology ready to applaud the studies showing that by adding our extraordinary hormone, medroxyprogesterone acetate (Provera), we have decreased the likelihood of uterine cancer? Will the people believe us? Are public relations experts certain that we can sell the people in the land, especially the women, on the idea that conjugated estrogens and synthetic estrogens offer the best hope for preventing osteoporosis, heart disease, and Alzheimer's disease? And that the risk of cancer pales in comparison?" asked the Medical Monarch, turning all of these annoying details over and over in his mind. He wanted everyone to know that he understood the issues involved. "Of course," he told himself, "I do not want them to think I do not fully recognize the superiority of the extraordinary hormones. They must be persuaded that my only difficulty is explaining the research to those who are actually unfit to be medical doctors or who are very foolish."

The Lords of the Bedchamber carried the imaginary train flowing from the Emperor's garments. They pretended to lift the train from the ground as though they were carrying it on each end. Certainly the Lords of the Bedchamber were not about to let anyone think that they were foolish or unfit for the position that they held.

The men and women heading the Departments of Obstetrics and Gynecology promoted the use of a chemically altered, patentable progesterone, Provera (medroxyprogesterone acetate, a progestin). The studies presented by the Medical Monarch showed that progestins have protective properties that decrease the likelihood of

cancer in those women with a uterus. The physicians did not
worry themselves with the likelihood of other cancers or with
the mound of disturbing information concerning the use of
Provera (warnings about breast cancer, facial hair growth,
depression, cardiovascular disease, liver disorders, and other
problems) published in the Physicians' Desk Reference.

They also continued to promote (with the help of the
unusually deceitful Pharmaceutical Princes and their public
relations experts) the use of conjugated estrogens (Premarin)
as the best hope for preventing osteoporosis, heart disease,
and Alzheimer's disease.

They could never let anyone think they could not understand the superiority of Premarin and Provera over bio-identical hormones, which have molecular structures exactly the
same as those in the human body. They could never for a
moment do that because the Pharmaceutical Princes and the
Medical Monarch agreed that conjugated estrogens
(Premarin), synthetic estrogen (ethinyl estradiol), and progestin (Provera) are clearly superior to the simple, bio-identical hormones. Of course, that great revelation cannot be
understood by anyone who is unfit to be a medical doctor or
who is very foolish. The physicians thought, "We could never
for a moment let anyone think that we are unfit for our
positions."

So the Emperor, sheltered under his high canopy,
walked in the very center of the procession, right
through the streets of his capital city, dressed (or
rather undressed) in his new clothes. All the people
standing along the route of the procession and those
looking out of the windows in the tall buildings
cried out, "Your Majesty the Emperor is wearing
such beautiful new clothes! The train is magnificent!" In fact, none of the people watching the
grand procession would admit that he or she could
not see the Emperor's new clothes. "Everyone else
in the kingdom sees these clothes and thinks that
they are beautiful," they reasoned, "I must not
admit that the Emperor's clothes are not visible to

*me, or I will be declared unfit for the position that
I hold or be considered very foolish!"*

So, the Medical Monarch continued to publicize and promote the research data supporting the benefits of the extraordinary hormones developed by the unusually deceptive Pharmaceutical Princes. All of the experts, who had actually read the studies themselves, and all of the people, who read the press releases outlining the significant points in the research studies, cried out, "These studies are both significant and conclusive. We now have further evidence that these extraordinary hormones offer outstanding benefits to women. It is perfectly clear that these hormones are safe and effective, and they offer women the best hope for overcoming the symptoms of menopause and preventing the diseases that plague women over fifty." In fact, very few physicians, and very few people in the general population, would admit that it was not perfectly clear why the hormones were so very beneficial. How could they be beneficial, in light of the fact that many women experienced side effects and/or became ill with life-threatening diseases? Although the people did not hear a lot about the report in the New England Journal of Medicine, the word "cancer" stuck in their minds. Nonetheless, who wanted to think about endometrial carcinoma, and who, in the general population, really understood the development of conjugated estrogens? Most important, few people in the general population and only a small percentage of the physicians in the land, knew that safe and effective hormones (identical to the molecular structures of those hormones that are made by the human body) were an option. Few people in the general population and only a small percentage of the physicians would admit that it was not at all clear that Premarin and Provera were perfectly, or even relatively, safe. Nor would they admit that they did not understand exactly why the conjugated estrogens and the synthetic compounds offered the best hope to women over fifty for preventing osteoporosis, heart disease, and Alzheimer's disease. They did not want to admit any of those things for fear they would be called unenlightened, unintelligent, uninformed, foolish, or unfit to be medical doctors.

Never before had the Emperor's clothes caused this kind of excitement. Then, after the procession was well underway, a child stepped up to the ropes that held the crowd back from the Royal Procession. No one wanted to admit not being able to see the Emperor's clothes for fear of being considered foolish or unfit for the position that he or she held. But the child had no fear, and once the Emperor came clearly into his view, he said, "The Emperor has on no clothes at all!" Immediately his father spoke up, "The child is telling the truth!" People all up and down the route of the procession repeated the words of the child until everyone in the streets and in the buildings knew what the child had said. Then they all began to yell the words out together: "The Emperor has on no clothes at all!"

Never before had any of the Medical Monarch's new medicines or research studies created so much interest as these had. The Medical Monarch and the Pharmaceutical Princes had marketed Premarin so well that it had become the most prescribed drug in the land. By 1975 approximately six million women in the country used Premarin.

Then, in 1978 a physician from Sebastopol, California, John R. Lee, M.D., heard a lecture on the subject of natural (bio-identical) progesterone by biochemist Ray Peat, Ph.D. In 1979 Dr. Lee began researching and prescribing natural progesterone. First, he began treating his patients suffering from osteoporosis with progesterone. Rather than delaying bone loss (by restraining osteoclast function), as does estrogen, he discovered that progesterone actually builds bone (by stimulating osteoblast function).[11]

During his years of clinical practice, John R. Lee, M.D., became known as "an expert on the clinical uses of natural progesterone."[12] Not only did he discover that natural progesterone, with or without estrogen, restores osteoblast function; he concluded that natural progesterone "is an essential factor in the prevention and proper treatment of osteoporosis."[13]

Throughout his years of practice, he came to recognize that natural progesterone is a "remarkably effective, safe, *and relatively inexpensive therapy for a wide range of female disorders resulting from estrogen dominance."[14] Although most of his colleagues applauded his presentations of clinical data, most did not choose to "apply the treatment to their patients. Their reasons were weak and self-serving, it seemed . . . invoking the fear of malpractice, their liability if perchance one of their patients developed a cancer, their concern about what colleagues might think, and the fact that no pharmaceutical company had undertaken to sponsor the treatment."[15] The physicians needed some official sanction before using natural progesterone (which has no known side effects) instead of synthetic progestin, which has numerous potential side effects—many of which are life-threatening and all of which are listed in the* Physicians' Desk Reference. *Dr. Lee discovered that most physicians had a "remarkable ignorance of hormone physiology."[16]*

Dr. Lee and others recognized the work of Dr. Katharina Dalton in London, who defined premenstrual syndrome and treated it successfully with high-dose progesterone suppositories.[17] Dr. Joel Hargrove of Vanderbilt University Medical Center published results indicating a 90 percent success rate as a result of treating PMS patients with oral progesterone.[18]

Christiane Northrup, M.D., a holistic physician and member of the Natural Healing Health Advisory Board, recommended an ERT alternative developed by Pharmacist Joseph Delk and Dr. Joel Hargrove that contains natural estrogen (estradiol, 0.5 mg) combined with natural progesterone (100 mg). "It is also available at lower doses. Women on this preparation do not get periods, as it maintains an inactive endometrium with none of the side effects of progestin."[19]

Some people began enjoying the benefits of natural hormones (bio-identical hormones) in the 1970s, but only a small percentage of the population had access to the information and services they required. Fifteen years of clinical practice proved to John R. Lee, M.D., that natural progesterone reverses osteoporosis and offers women in industrialized countries the only solution to the problems they face as a result of estrogen dominance.[20] At sixty, Dr. Lee retired from his medi-

*cal practice to share his knowledge by writing and speaking
on the multiple roles of natural progesterone. The Revolution
was well underway by the time his first book went to press in
1993, but still, very few people had access to vital information
concerning hormone balance. When Dr. Lee shared his knowledge and experience, he realized his words were "very inflammatory. I was challenging what the pharmaceutical industry was saying. I was challenging what was being taught
in medical school."[21] He considered conventional medicine to
be dysfunctional and unenlightened, and the use of chemically altered hormones (analogues) to be irresponsible. "With
each alteration of the molecule it becomes a different molecule."[22] Dr. Lee came to regard as supreme arrogance on
the part of the pharmaceutical industry their decision to change
the construction of progesterone (which has no side effects),
and to make a progestin (with a long list of life-threatening
side effects). He found it incredible that they sold the progestin as though it were essentially the same as progesterone.
"The typical doctors only know about these (progestins).
They don't even know that natural progesterone exists. And
yet it has been out in creams for years."[23]*

*John R. Lee, M.D., continued speaking out against the
use of synthetic steroids throughout the last decade of the
twentieth century. He was joined by Neal Barnard, M.D.,
president of the Physicians Committee for Responsible Medicine, and a host of other men and women who distributed Dr.
John R. Lee's books and/or prescribed natural progesterone
transdermal cream to their patients.*

*In the 1980s Jonathan V. Wright, M.D., pioneered with a
prescription that came to be known as triple estrogen or "tri-
est." His pharmacist (and friend), Ed Thorpe, compounded
(to Wright's specifications) estrone, estradiol, and estriol in
the pattern which mimics the circulating estrogens in our
bodies.[24] John R. Lee, M.D., spoke to the hearts and minds
of a number of health professionals when he issued a challenge in 1993. He urged medical doctors to muster the "con-
fidence and will power to act in the best tradition of being a
physician scientist and a strong advocate for your patients."[25]*

Other physicians and researchers began making an impact telling the simple truth regarding natural hormone therapy. Included in that esteemed group are Alan Gaby, M.D., Ward Dean, M.D., Betty Kamen, Ph.D., David Zava, Ph.D., and Marcus Laux, N.D.

The Emperor knew immediately that the people were telling the truth and that he had been foolish indeed. He felt ridiculous, but that didn't change his outward behavior. He had learned how to hold on to his dignity as the Emperor. He turned to the Lords of the Bedchamber and directed their actions: "We have started the procession. Let us continue just as we have planned." So the Lords of the Bedchamber took extreme care not to let the imaginary train hit the ground. They walked on with their heads held high. They continued to pretend that they were holding the Emperor's long train. And they continued to pretend that they were smoothing the wrinkles from the Emperor's new clothes. They all continued the procession that had been planned in order to show off the Emperor's new clothes—even though the Emperor had on no clothes at all.

The Medical Monarch knew the people who were acting in the best tradition of medicine and science were telling the truth, and he was foolish indeed. He felt ridiculous when he allowed himself to think about it, but that didn't change his outward behavior. He had learned how to hold on to his power and dignity. "Money and marketing will suppress the news for a while," he thought to himself, "even the sort of news that could change the course of people's lives."

The Pharmaceutical Princes began complaining to the Medical Monarch about cable television, alternative radio, the Internet, newsletters, books, special interest periodicals, and other sources of information about hormone therapy. "There's more and more talk about bio-identical hormones. The credentials of our well-known physicians and surgeons simply don't impress everyone. Nobody on our side is having the impact of

Dr. Robert A. Wilson. Those were the days! Nobody could even buy progesterone cream then. Now, the stuff is actually tested and certified in order to protect consumers."[26]

The Medical Monarch had heard enough. "We started a successful media campaign three decades ago. We will continue it just as we have planned." So, the unusually deceptive Pharmaceutical Princes took another look at some of the studies they had planned and continued to pretend that they were scholarly and scientific. They continued to pretend they were advancing medicine and science. They continued to pretend that there were only two alternatives. First, women could take conjugated estrogens and synthetic compounds (ERT or HRT), and overcome the symptoms of hormonal imbalance (accepting the fact that hormone therapy carries with it the risk of disease). Or second, women could refuse ERT or HRT as a means of overcoming the symptoms of hormonal imbalance (thereby accepting the increased risk of suffering from osteoporosis and memory loss, and of dying from heart disease). No matter how many books and articles presented other options, they continued to pretend there were only these two alternatives.

Then, many years later . . .

. . . sometime after the turn of the century, in the year two thousand and something . . . compounding pharmacies were commonplace. Membership in the American College for the Advancement in Medicine exploded. Oldways Preservation and Exchange Trust Conferences became more popular than rock concerts.

Millions of people, with named and no-name degenerative diseases, decided to make it their business to learn to get well. And the New York Times dug out the thirty-page Special Edition on Women's Health that they had published many years earlier on Sunday, 21 June 1998. The New York Times confessed its failure to print the whole truth regarding hormonal imbalance. They issued a new thirty-page Special Edition on Women's Health containing these headlines:

*"Safe and Effective Bio-Identical Hormones
Have Been Available for Decades"*

"Estrogen Deficiency Is Largely a Myth"

"Progesterone Deficiency Is Real"

*"Physicians Aren't Measuring
Biologically Active Progesterone"*

*"Conjugated Estrogens and Synthetic
Compounds Are Beneficial Only to
the People Who Are Selling Them"*

*"Saliva, Not Plasma, Represents the
Bio-Active Levels of
Endogenous Hormones"*

*"The Major Cause of Progesterone
Deficiency Is Follicle Depletion
Secondary to Xenobiotics"*

*"Diet and Bio-Cultural Differences
Aren't the Only Causes of Hormonal
Imbalance in the Industrialized World—
Xenobiotics Are at the Heart of the Problem"*

*Finally, the truth won out—on that particular issue. The
Medical Monarch and the Pharmaceutical Princes dreamed
up other medicines for all of the other degenerative diseases.
But they had to stop telling people that conjugated estrogens
and synthetic compounds were beneficial in any way, because no one in the land wanted to hear it. People yelled out
the news and danced in the streets. "There are safe and
effective solutions for hormonal imbalance. Natural progesterone and bio-identical estrogens are widely available! We
now have hundreds of thousands of health practitioners trained
and ready to give us the help we need!"*

Notes

1. Andrew Purvis, "Cheaper Can Be Better: A Study Comparing
Heart Medications Raises Questions about High-Pressure Tactics
in Drug Marketing," *Time*, 18 March 1991, 70.

2. John R. Lee, M.D., *Natural Progesterone: The Multiple Roles of a Remarkable Hormone,* Revised ed. (Sebastopol, CA: BLL Publishing, 1993, 1997), 25.

3. GAO (General Accounting Office) Report (Washington, DC, 1990).

4. Purvis, "Cheaper Can Be Better," 70.

5. Ibid.

6. Marcus Laux, N.D., and Christine Conrad, *Natural Woman, Natural Menopause* (New York: HarperCollins Publishers, 1997), 44-45.

7. Robert A. Wilson, M.D., *Feminine Forever* (New York: Evans and Company, 1966).

8. Ibid., 211-212.

9. Ibid., 207.

10. H.K. Ziel, and W.D. Finkle, "Increased Risk of Endometrial Carcinoma among Users of Conjugated Estrogens," *New England Journal of Medicine* 293, no. 23 (1975): 1167-1170.

11. John R. Lee, M.D., with David T. Zava, Ph.D., *The Secrets of Natural Hormone Therapy: Keys to Preventing Women's Most Serious Health Problems* (Harry DeLigter Productions, 1996), two audio cassettes.

12. Christiane Northrup, M.D., *Women's Bodies, Women's Wisdom: Creating Physical and Emotional Health and Healing* (New York: Bantam Books, 1994; Bantam Trade Paperback Edition, 1995), 165.

13. Lee, *Natural Progesterone,* 69.

14. Ibid., 87.

15. Ibid., iii.

16. Ibid.

17. Ibid., 50.

18. Ibid., 52.

19. Northrup, *Women's Bodies,* 686.

20. Lee, with Zava, *Natural Hormone Therapy,* audio cassettes.

21. Ibid.

22. Ibid.

23. Ibid.

24. Jonathan V. Wright, M.D., and John Morgenthaler, *Natural Hormone Replacement for Women over Forty-Five* (Petaluma, CA: Smart Publications, 1997), 43.

25. Lee, *Natural Progesterone,* iii.

26. Aeron LifeCycles Product Integrity Certification Program, 1933 Davis Street, Suite 310, San Leandro, CA 94577 Telephone 1-800-631-7900.

———————————————— Part Three

Who Is Suffering from Estrogen Dominance?

• The Big Story: What is estrogen dominance? What are the symptoms of estrogen dominance? What are the causes? Why are women in the industrialized countries most affected?
• How can women safely and effectively overcome hot flashes, night sweats, vaginal pain, bloating, and weight gain?
• Protocols using bio-identical hormones

Preface to the Big Story

My own experiences, the histories of my patients, and the science that is pertinent, prospective, and randomized, leave me deeply skeptical that menopause is a medical liability and most of all that estrogen deficiency is the major problem.

—Jerilynn C. Prior, M.D.,
"One Voice on Menopause,"
JAMWA 49, no. 1

Dr. Prior is an associate professor of medicine, Division of Endocrinology at the University of British Columbia in Vancouver, Canada. She has written a number of important papers. In the article referenced above, Dr. Prior tells what happened to her after being invited to write a short chapter about osteoporosis to be included in a monograph for family doctors on menopause treatment. When she asked the editor ("a young academic gynecologist") for guidelines, she soon realized her real assignment was to write that all menopausal women need estrogen treatment. Since that was not her view, she expressed her thoughts and discussed why her information would be helpful for doctors and the patients they served.

> It was no use. He was unshakable. His message was truth: *Menopause is an estrogen deficiency disease and must be treated with estrogen.* I have both a clear idea of what I am experiencing as a perimenopausal woman and a scientific understanding of reproductive endocrinology. Yet, my experiences are dismissed since they don't fit the current notion. He is not the only one who is certain of the menopause truth. So are other influential physicians.[1]

In spite of Dr. Prior's personal experiences as a perimenopausal woman, and her scientific understanding of reproductive endocrinology, she was quickly silenced by those who held the dominant view favoring estrogen therapy. That someone with her credentials, with research on her side, can be so easily dismissed, underscores the magnitude of the challenge that women face. The following menopausal dilemma characterizes the view of Dr. Prior's editor, a view that depicts perimenopausal or menopausal women, who suffer from hormonal imbalance, as being estrogen deficient and in need of conjugated estrogen for life. Clearly, it is not my view. Nor is it the view of many respected physicians and scientists worldwide. However, the following well-financed point of view dominates the media, the market, and the medical schools.

1. The mid-life female body gradually produces an insufficient amount of estrogen, as cycles become longer and scant.

2. Menopausal women need estrogen treatment to prevent osteoporosis and heart disease.

3. The risk of endometrial cancer, as a result of estrogen replacement therapy or hormone replacement therapy (estrogen plus progestin or progesterone), is small compared to the disease risk as a result of not taking estrogen.

4. The risk of heart disease, as a result of an estrogen deficiency at menopause and during the postmenopausal period, is great.

What had Dr. Prior's personal experiences taught her? She understood exactly what millions of other women know about their own perimenopausal experiences: Symptoms of perimenopause are more like adolescence than postmenopause. And just as in journeys through adolescence, the woman in midlife may encounter a variety of symptoms resulting from hormonal imbalance. But is the imbalance caused from estrogen deficiency? Like many perimenopausal women, Dr. Prior had hot flashes and night sweats without missing one period. Her cycles were normal or short in interval, and heavy in flow. Her cycles had a normal luteal phase length of ten or more days.

> What if I had told this editor that I believe I am currently experiencing estrogen excess! Otherwise, I find it hard to explain my short follicular phases, early and increased cervical mucus production, short cycles, breast enlargement, and nipple tenderness.[2]

In Dr. Prior's article, she cites numerous other researchers who have reached the same conclusions. And she asks a simple question: How is it that breast tenderness, weight gain, bloating, and mood changes (when experienced by an adolescent female) signal high estrogen levels, while the same symptoms experienced by a female during midlife are read as symptoms of estrogen deficiency? The sobering truth that leaps from the pages of this journal article is that the arrogance and ignorance that silenced Jerilynn Prior runs rampant in the medical profession.

Although this 1994 article by Jerilynn Prior, M.D., does not contain important answers, she is asking all the right questions! She says early in the article "I am the first to admit that I am not a menopause expert." She goes on to say:

> I am only a perimenopausal woman with 15 years of practice in reproductive endocrinology who has conducted (and been able to publish a few) prospective studies of reproduction.[3]

I do not offer this article as an explanation of, or answer to, estrogen dominance. I find this article so very compelling, because it typifies the plight of an inquiring and conscientious physician. This story is significant because Dr. Prior is an accomplished physician. If she cannot be heard, then what will it take to overcome those who stand against irresponsible medicine? It will take educated consumers, who know what constitutes appropriate health care, and who will demand that their physicians practice responsible medicine. The Physicians Committee for Responsible Medicine is one good place for physicians, and consumers of medical services, to begin.

The oppression has gone on for decades. Now, many more physicians are speaking out and seeking the education they did not get in medical school (and cannot get from the pharmaceutical representatives!). Many physicians do want to know how to prevent and cure degenerative disease and are disheartened, after acquiring an expensive medical education, to discover that they have not even begun a meaningful inquiry. As we discuss the lifework and crusade of John R. Lee, M.D., we will see a model of a physician who educated himself after (and in spite of) medical school. We can also learn from his battles, because they are, in fact, our battles as well.

Before I leave the story of Jerilynn C. Prior, M.D., I should relate another aspect of the conversation she had with the editor who rejected her views. Any number of well-informed/well-intentioned medical doctors could have written the script.

Dr. Prior expressed her concern about the "currently favored continuous 0.625 mg conjugated estrogen schedule with 2.5 mg of medroxyprogesterone."[4] The low progestin dose, in her opinion, would not prevent the increased risk of endometrial cancer. The physician-editor agreed that it probably would not, and he cited a paper by A.T. Leather ("Endometrial Histology and Bleeding Patterns after Eight Years of Continuous Combined Estrogen and Progestin Therapy in Postmenopausal Women"[5]) showing that two out of forty-four women on a similar continuous schedule developed cancer. Dr. Prior said that she hadn't seen it and thanked him for the reference. The rest of her account is chilling.

No one who understands the problems with synthetic compounds would regard Dr. Prior's protocol as the best choice for women. However, it is an improvement, a vast improvement, over standard practice. If some readers imagine that things have changed since the date of Dr. Prior's article, they have only to talk to women about the advice they are being given by their physicians. I speak to women all across America, in large cities and in small communities. They cannot get competent advice. They find themselves face to face with physicians, male and female, who are building their medical "businesses" and do not have the time, or the inclination, to continue their education. They learned certain practices and procedures in medical school. They understand what is acceptable. They do not want to risk their reputations or their standing with peers.

As readers examine the protocols at the end of this section, they will find safe and effective protocols used by enlightened physicians. Consider the current situation: Safe and effective solutions to hormonal imbalance are available, and only a small band of health professionals are willing and able to prescribe them. Consumers must come alive on this issue and be heard.

Dr. Prior's story is important because even these minimal improvements in standard protocols would not be tolerated. The pharmaceutical industry and the medical community have a grip on our lives. I predict that women across America, from the political left to the political right, will join hands on this issue.

Dr. Prior's recommendation to her colleagues is of course a far safer protocol than the protocols in standard practice. Here is the schedule that she details in her article (and suggested to the journal editor who silenced her):

1. Patients should increase the dosage of medroxyprogesterone from 2.5 mg a day to 10 mg a day and take it on a continuous schedule.

2. Patients should lower the dosage of conjugated estrogen from 0.635 mg per day to 0.3 mg a day.

3. Patients should not take the conjugated estrogen on a continuous schedule, but rather take it on a cyclic schedule (0.3 mg for twenty-five days each month).[6]

Dr. Prior urged her colleague to consider a more reasonable and safer protocol based on the following points:

1. Most women want to avoid menstrual flow and this protocol would accomplish that.

2. The higher dose of progestin would eliminate the risk of endometrial cancer.

3. The lower (0.3 mg) and cyclic dose of conjugated estrogen would have the same positive spinal bone effect as 0.625 mg conjugated estrogen taken daily without a progestin.

4. "I think women who already have low bone densities need progestin in addition to estrogen in order to promote new bone formation."[7] Dr. Prior's research on this topic is impressive (J.C. Prior, "Progesterone As a Bone-Trophic Hormone," *Endocrine Reviews* 11, no. 2). [Dr. Dorian's note: Readers will find comments in this section by John R. Lee, M.D. and Neal Barnard, M.D. (president of the Physicians Committee for Responsible Medicine) concerning the hazards of progestins. The protocols using bio-identical hormones, listed at the end of this section, offer safe alternatives to any schedule involving Premarin and Provera.]

Dr. Prior tells us the editor's response to this safer and more reasonable protocol with an exact quotation:

"I'm not so sure you should write that. You would confuse family doctors. And it's not a well-accepted schedule. The 0.625 mg continuous Premarin and low dose Provera schedule is the one that is accepted."[8]

When is the lie so big that we believe it?

. . . when pride and self-interest demand that those who speak the truth be silenced.

In Dr. Prior's article she speaks of herself with humility and restraint. She ends the article with the thoughts that came to her just after her telephone conversation with the editor. She states concisely what his actions really mean and then asks the reader a most challenging question:

> As I put the phone down, I mused: At least this time
> I had had a fighting chance to get across a different

view of menopause. I knew the booklet editor, and he knew of my work. I was even asked to write the chapter. Yet, despite all of these factors in my favor, I was not heard. Although I am chronologically his senior and academically his peer, I have been given no say.

If my voice can be so easily and effectively silenced, are other women likely to be heard?[9]

Men, women, and children are directly impacted by estrogen dominance. There is a grassroots movement underway. Dr. John R. Lee refers to this outcry as "the revolution." (On the audiotape we hear him chuckle.) Many feminists have been in denial regarding the health crises that the overwhelming majority of women in the western industrialized world face during midlife, after midlife, and/or in the childbearing years. They are right to protest the medicalization of menopause. They are right to renounce menopause as a disease. They are right to reject conjugated estrogen, synthetic estrogen, and synthetic progesterone (progestin). But it is dishonest to deny that women are suffering from PMS or to regard hot flashes as "power surges." Hot flashes and night sweats are positive only if we pay attention to them as warning signals. These symptoms indicate that our bodies are out of balance and consequently running low on strength and power. If we are to celebrate every cycle of life, as indeed we should, we acknowledge signs of degeneration and learn how to regenerate our bodies.

The discomforts of PMS, and the distress that women feel during perimenopause, menopause, and postmenopause, simply tell us that our current dietary and lifestyle regimens are not solving our problems. Most women in America need to start there. The vast majority of Americans, including many of the journalists who write and speak on the topic of health, don't understand what constitutes an optimal dietary regimen. I suggest that readers consider the epidemiological studies and ask the most basic questions: Who are the healthiest people in the world? And why? (See Part Six.) If we understand the connection between dietary and lifestyle habits, and hormonal imbalance, we have taken the first giant leap. We can begin to solve our problems.

If we then look to the lives and ways of women in other cultures, who don't have our problems, we gain hope and courage. If we are willing to investigate and acknowledge the dangers we face from petrochemicals (xenobiotics), we are more likely to do what it is in our power to do to protect ourselves from harm. Health is a continuum. Menopausal distress, premenstrual syndrome, and the symptoms of andropause alert us to the fact that we are in a degenerative state. We need to pay attention to our bodies, learn how to live better and longer, and begin walking in the direction of wellness.

Apart from the dietary and lifestyle choices that make Americans the world leaders in degenerative disease (see Part Six: Who Are the Healthiest People in the World? And Why?), there are other reasons for hormonal imbalance. Women are not the only ones falling apart. Men of all ages, and children of all ages, are also in crisis. Feminists, Betty Friedan among them, have politicized menopause. Marcus Laux, N.D., and Christine Conrad discuss this point in their book, *Natural Woman, Natural Menopause* (HarperCollins). Feminists have come out against HRT, as though the only problems we have are those imagined by physicians, who are fabricating symptoms and making menopause a disease. Many feminists have ignored, or minimized, the real and enormous challenges that men, women, and children face as a result of environmental estrogens. The role of petrochemical derivatives in the problem of estrogen dominance is undeniable.

Those of us who understand the absurdity of taking conjugated estrogen, synthetic estrogen, and synthetic progesterone (progestin), and who have paid careful attention to dietary and lifestyle choices for decades, are not afraid to face the real problems that exist for men, women, and children. If we deny the existence of problems associated with hormonal imbalance, we become as dishonest as the medical industrial complex that finds ways to profit from problems, rather than to solve them.

The Big Story

What is estrogen dominance? What are the symptoms of estrogen dominance? What are the causes? Why are women in the industrialized countries most affected?

In order to understand estrogen dominance, it is important to think through the issues explored in Part Two of this book: The Big Lie. When Is the Truth So Obvious We Cannot See It? Clearly, when the estrogen in the body is not in proper balance with progesterone, when estrogen levels are higher than is desirable, it is accurate to say that estrogen becomes the dominant hormone. To understand why this is a major problem, we need to understand the physiological effects of both estrogen and progesterone.

John R. Lee, M.D., is a central figure in what I call the Big Story. On the cover of his book, *What Your Doctor May Not Tell You about Menopause* (Warner Books), Christiane Northrup, M.D. (author of *Women's Bodies, Women's Wisdom*) has this to say about Dr. Lee:

> John Lee has pioneered work in women's health that has greatly influenced and enhanced the way I practice medicine.

It can now be said that many, many physicians have been greatly influenced and have changed the way they practice medicine as a result of the work of John R. Lee. Twenty-three years after graduating from medical school and in his twentieth year of family practice, Dr. Lee heard a lecture on natural progesterone by Ray Peat, Ph.D., of Oregon. The year was 1978. Lee had been invited to deliver a report to the Orthomolecular Medical Society in San Francisco. In an audio tape recorded before a live audience, Dr. Lee describes Ray Peat as "quite a guy . . . one of those geniuses . . . not all that easy to pretend to be normal."[10] In this same audio message, Dr. Lee shares his history and his cause. Dr. Lee mentions organizations that provide continuing education and offer a forum for inquiring individuals. This information helps us to get beyond the unprincipled practices of many leaders in the

medical community and pharmaceutical industry, and to learn
from those professionals who are interested in the prevention
and cure of degenerative disease.

John Lee won a scholarship to Harvard, was in the top
third of his class every year, and graduated with honors. He is
a graduate of the University of Minnesota Medical School.
During his years of practice in Mill Valley, California, he
served as Chairman of the Marin County Medical Society
Environmental Health Committee and Clinical Instructor in
Medicine at the University of California Medical School in
San Francisco. His articles have been published in *The New
England Journal of Medicine* and other medical journals. Dr.
Lee has devoted years to the study of optimal health and the
prevention of degenerative disease. After being "a regular doc-
tor" for ten years, he learned that his training didn't help
people to stay well.[11]

> I began going to alternative medicine meetings—ACAM
> [American College for Advancement in Medicine] and
> Orthomolecular Medical Society—and I found them
> much more interesting, much more challenging; and, in
> fact, the level of intelligence of the doctors there was
> considerably higher than at the regular meetings.[12]

Lee also expressed his thoughts concerning the limitations
of medical school before the same live audience:

> Medical school is a kind of trade school—you learn how
> to do things and you learn how to regurgitate answers
> that the professor wants you to give . . . It's not a school
> where you go to really study the philosophical and bio-
> logical and chemical unknowns. The attraction of medi-
> cine to me was all the unknowns. It's a living, continu-
> ing, evolving science with a whole lot of things we don't
> understand.[13]

Fifteen years of clinical practice proved to John Lee many
truths about progesterone. He retired and wrote a book at the
age of sixty "to shorten the learning curve for other people."[14]
The book, *Natural Progesterone: The Multiple Roles of a Remarkable Hormone,* simply explains, in technical, medical lan-

guage, everything he has learned about progesterone and hormonal balance. Lee's work cannot be dismissed. But it presents a problem for those who ought to be telling this Big Story to the women in America. Physicians who encounter John Lee's work know that they did not acquire Lee's knowledge in medical school, nor in lectures, nor in textbooks. And they are not getting Lee's information from the pharmaceutical advertisements. Consequently, many physicians found his work "very inflammatory."[15]

> I was challenging what the pharmaceutical companies were saying. I was challenging what was being taught in medical school.[16]

It is important to note that John Lee states that the turning point in his life and medical practice came as a result of two events:

The first event, the release of an article in the *New England Journal of Medicine*, showed the risks of unopposed estrogen. (H.K. Ziel, M.D., and W.D. Finkle, Ph.D. "Increased Risk of Endometrial Carcinoma among Users of Conjugated Estrogens." *New England Journal of Medicine*, no. 23, 1975).

Note that the sale of Premarin (manufactured by Ayerst Laboratories) quadrupled in the United States between 1962 and 1973. Certainly, the promotional work of Robert A. Wilson, M.D. (highlighted in Part Two) contributed greatly to the sale of Premarin during that period.

When important information about estrogen came to light in the seventies, John R. Lee stopped in his tracks. What did the pharmaceutical industry and the medical community do when the dangers of unopposed estrogen were exposed? Marcus Laux, N.D. and Christine Conrad explain:

> The dosages of Premarin were lowered, and based on studies showing that the addition of a synthetic progesterogenic substance, a *progestin*, decreased the likelihood of uterine cancer in women, those women with an intact uterus were given Provera with the Premarin. Women without a uterus, it was decided, didn't need the "protective" properties of progesterone, as lacking a

uterus eliminated the risk of endometrial cancer. Which, of course, is true, but what about *other cancers?* And the necessary *balancing* effect of progesterone on estrogen? What about the other possible risks of unopposed estrogen?[17]

John R. Lee explains in some detail the response of the medical community to this issue of unopposed estrogen:

> In the mid-seventies, a Mayo Clinic consensus conference concluded that estrogen should never be given to any woman with an intact uterus (any woman who hasn't had a hysterectomy) without also giving progesterone or a progestin as protection from endometrial cancer. The effect of this was to expand the market for progestins to include *all* women, whether menstruating or postmenopausal! The financial implications of this are difficult to exaggerate.
>
> Even the threat of breast cancer has not stopped the market for estrogen/progestin hormone therapy. A 1989 report by Leif Bergkvist et al. convincingly showed that supplemental estrogen (at least estradiol) when combined with a progestin "seems to be associated with a slightly *increased* risk of breast cancer, which is not prevented and may even be *increased* by the addition of the progestins" (emphasis added). This has not slowed the progestin bandwagon. Meanwhile, natural progesterone, as we shall see in a later chapter can help *prevent* breast cancer.
>
> Women should be upset that the hormone "balancing" being done to them uses synthetic and abnormal versions of the real goods, when the natural hormones are available, safer, and more appropriate to their bodies.[18]

In the 1970s, while the medical community promoted the synthetic compounds produced by the pharmaceutical industry, John Lee began practicing medicine differently.

The second event that marked the turning point in John R. Lee's life and medical practice came when he began experimenting using natural progesterone with patients for whom estrogen was contraindicated. He learned many things from his patients with osteoporosis:

1. Patients have excessive bone loss;
   OR
2. Some patients do not have enough new bone formation;
   OR
3. Patients may have both excessive bone loss and inadequate new bone formation.

Bone loss occurs before the loss of estrogen. Our bone density peaks at age thirty-five and begins to decline sharply at age fifty-five. What causes bone loss at age thirty-five? The answer most often is low levels of progesterone. But why are women experiencing progesterone deficiencies well before midlife? That discussion follows.

Here is what Dr. Lee's clinical work revealed about osteoporosis:

1. Patients not on hormones experienced 1½ percent bone loss per year and 4½ percent loss in three years.
2. Patients on estrogen experienced no change in bone density.
3. Patients on progesterone experienced 15 percent more bone in three years!

This has never been reported before with any other treatment. Progesterone is absolutely safe. When patients use progesterone, bone building occurs with or without estrogen. Dr. Lee has been talking about this for twenty years. Dr. Lee says that this should have started a revolution. Still in good humor he adds, "I'm getting a little tired of the revolution."[19]

Dr. Lee recommends that any diagnostic or treatment program for osteoporosis begin with a bone mineral density (B.M.D.) measurement. The patient and the physician need a baseline with which to evaluate the results of the treatment. He suggests that all women measure their height when they are thirty and continue to measure their height yearly. When the spinal bone deterioration causes a loss in height, it usually indicates osteoporosis. As Dr. Lee discusses in his books, osteoporosis is a multifactorial disease. Progesterone without proper diet, nutrients, and exercise is not a proper protocol for the prevention or reversal of osteoporosis.[20]

What Is Progesterone?

The ovaries of menstruating women produce progesterone and estrogen. Progesterone is made just prior to ovulation. Progesterone increases rapidly after ovulation and becomes the major female gonadal hormone during the latter two weeks of the menstrual cycle. Progesterone and estrogen are made in the adrenal glands. Progesterone is also made in the testes of the male.

If we picture the biosynthetic pathway for gonadal hormones as a sequence of activities, we can easily understand the way in which progesterone participates in the ultimate formation of estrogens, testosterone, and corticosteroids.

1. Every cell makes cholesterol.
2. From cholesterol we produce pregnenolone.
3. From pregnenolone we produce progesterone.
4. From progesterone we can start making the corticosteroids.
5. From the corticosteroids we make 17 hydroxyprogesterone.
6. From 17 hydroxyprogesterone we make androstenedione that produces testosterone, estrone, estradiol, and estriol.

What should consumers know about the alteration of the molecules? How different are synthetic estrogens and synthetic progesterone from the molecules that our bodies produce?

> With each alteration of the molecule, it becomes a different molecule. So it strikes me as supreme arrogance of the pharmaceutical companies to think that they can change the construction of progesterone and still sell it as though it were real progesterone.[21]

> With molecular shapes altered by the addition of atoms at unusual positions, synthetic steroids are not subject

to the usual metabolic control provided by our enzymes. Thus, their effects cannot be "tuned down" or "turned off," nor can these synthetic compounds be efficiently excreted by one's usual enzymatic mechanisms. Despite their advertisements, synthetic hormones are *not* equivalent to natural hormones.[22]

Common causes of estrogen dominance in western industrialized countries:

1. Estrogen replacement therapy
2. Birth control pills that have an excessive estrogen component
3. Hysterectomy (can induce subsequent ovary dysfunction or atrophy)
4. Obesity during the menopausal and postmenopausal periods
5. Early follicle depletion during premenopause, resulting in a lack of ovulation and thus lack of progesterone well before the onset of menopause
6. Exposure to xenoestrogens (cause of early follicle depletion)

John R. Lee offers us two especially useful lists that put the estrogen dominance problem in perspective: List one tells us the effect of both estrogen and progesterone.[23] List two gives us the symptoms caused or worsened by estrogen dominance.[24]

List One

Estrogen and Progesterone Effects
E=estrogen; P=progesterone

E causes breast stimulation
    P protects against fibrocystic breasts
E increases body fat
    P helps use fat for energy
E causes salt and fluid retention
    P is a natural antidepressant
E interferes with thyroid hormone
    P facilitates thyroid hormone action

E increases blood clotting
  P normalizes blood clotting
E decreases sex drive
  P restores sex drive
E impairs blood sugar control
  P normalizes blood sugar levels
E causes a loss of zinc and a retention of copper
  P normalizes zinc and copper levels

List Two

Symptoms caused or worsened by estrogen dominance:

Aging (an acceleration of the process)

Allergies

Autoimmune disorders (e.g., lupus erythematosus, thyroiditis, Sjögren's disease)

Blood clotting (increased)

Brain fog

Breast tenderness

Depression

Fat around the abdomen, hips, and thighs

Fatigue

Fibrocystic breasts

Gallbladder disease

Headaches

Hypoglycemia

Infertility

Irritability

Loss of libido

Memory loss

Miscarriage

Osteoporosis

Premenopausal bone loss

Premenstrual syndrome

Thyroid dysfunction mimicking hypothyroidism

Uterine cancer

Uterine fibroids

Water retention, bloating

What Are Xenobiotics?

Quite simply, they are petrochemical derivatives. These molecules from petrochemical sources contaminate the environment, the food chain, and the air that we breathe. They are all around us—in the out-gassing of carpet, spermicidal gels, spreading agents in salad dressings. Many of these substances act as estrogenic substances. Others are anti-estrogenic. The term xenobiotic is now used more often than xenoestrogen, because it covers a wider field.

We come in contact with xenoestrogens in food, particularly meat and dairy, with the heavy concentration of pesticide residue. The beef that we produce in America is, in the opinion of many experts, a threat to the health and well-being of those who consume it. The following comments are from an article written by Dr. Samuel S. Epstein, Professor of Environmental and Occupational Medicine at the University of Illinois School of Public Health and Chairman of the Cancer Prevention Coalition, Inc. in Chicago:

> The question we ought to be asking is not why Europe won't buy our hormone-treated meat, but why we allow beef from hormone-treated cattle to be sold to American and Canadian consumers . . . The endocrine-disruptive effects of estrogenic pesticides and other industrial food contaminants known as xenoestrogens are now under intensive investigation by federal regulatory agencies. But the contamination of meat with residues of the far more potent estradiol remains ignored.
>
> These hormones are linked ever more closely to the escalating incidence of reproductive cancers in the U.S. since 1950—55 percent for breast cancer, 120 percent for testicular cancer, and 190 percent for prostate cancer.[25]

Gasoline fumes and soft plastics are also sources of xenoestrogens. None of us should be subjected to gasoline fumes, and we should avoid being contaminated by plastics whenever possible. The clingy plastic wrap is the most hazardous. When we wrap our food with plastic, the chemicals in the plastic are absorbed by the food.

If we consume only organic meat and dairy, we eliminate the greatest source of xenoestrogens. The issue of how much protein we should consume from animal sources is the concern of Part Six. Many of us prefer a regimen free of all animal protein except for the omega-3 fatty acid rich cold water fish (salmon, sardines, and mackerel). Most Americans need to focus on an optimal dietary regimen that will reverse degenerative disease, because they have spent a number of years consuming processed, devitalized, high-fat, sugar-filled, chemical-laden foods.

If our diet does not contain phytoestrogens (plant estrogens) such as the isoflavones found in soybeans, or the lignans found in flaxseed, we have little protection from the xenoestrogens. The plant estrogens rescue us by occupying the estrogen receptor sites. (See Part Six regarding the dietary regimens of the healthiest people in the world.) John R. Lee explains what the xenoestrogens do:

> A hormone mimic such as a xenoestrogen may occupy the receptor and travel to the chromosome, to the DNA, and carry out a very potent estrogenic reaction. Or it may bind to the receptor, but yet be so different that the receptor will not accept it in that sense and nothing will happen.[26]

The point is that the xenoestrogen will cause an inappropriate hormonal response, or the xenoestrogen will block the normal hormone response. When our receptors are filled with these antagonists, our natural hormones are unable to work properly. How are xenoestrogens affecting human beings? We are responding to these petrochemical derivatives the same way that the alligators in Florida are responding. Female alligators aren't making eggs. They have large ovaries and follicles that are not functioning. Young women in the United States are not making eggs and not making progesterone. ~~This is why it is so important for even young women to have a hormone saliva test.~~ A low level of progesterone could cause infertility, premenstrual syndrome, autoimmune disease, miscarriage, ~~bone loss, and~~ many other disorders. Simple, non-invasive saliva testing is available.

[handwritten margin note: 3 mil eggs formed in a 3 month old fetus]

Young girls are entering puberty at earlier and earlier ages due to estrogen dominance. Men have been affected as well. Males in industrialized countries are producing sperm at a rate that is 50 percent lower than the rate of sperm production thirty-five years ago. Babies may look normal, then, in their thirties, the females may lose the ability to make progesterone, and the males the ability to make sperm.[27]

> We have a dysfunctional conventional medicine based on chemically altered hormones—analogues—and the typical doctors only know about these. They don't even know that natural ~~progesterone~~ exists and yet it's been out in these creams for years.
>
> We have to tell people that there's a problem. Progesterone deficiency exists. Estrogen deficiency is largely a myth. The problems that women are mostly hampered by—osteoporosis, breast cancer, decline in mental acuity, loss of libido—these are related to ~~progesterone~~. They are not estrogen problems.[28]

Dietary and lifestyle factors are the main determinants of health for those who want to prevent or reverse osteoporosis, heart disease, memory loss, PMS, and male menopause. Hormonal balance is essential in overcoming these and other degenerative diseases. Part Six and Part Seven of this book offer guidelines for building a foundation for optimal health. For more specific information, the audiotape series by the same title, *Hormonal Imbalance, the Madness and the Message,* covers in detail three topics not fully explored in this book. Male menopause (andropause or viropause), premenstrual syndrome (PMS), and safe ways for women over fifty to prevent and reverse osteoporosis are the subjects of three of the six audiotapes in that series.

Part Six (Who Are the Healthiest People in the World? And Why?) lays the foundation for the prevention and cure of degenerative disease. All of us need to know what constitutes an optimal dietary regimen, how to completely digest food and assimilate nutrients, how to avoid and overcome irritable bowel disease, how to manage Type I diabetes, and how to prevent and cure Type II diabetes.

Protocols Using Bio-identical Hormones

> The major cause of progesterone deficiency among women in western industrialized countries is follicle depletion, secondary to xenobiotics.[29]

For those women who are suffering from estrogen dominance, Dr. Lee recommends a low dose of natural progesterone (20 to 25 mg) twice a day. This is a physiologic dose. He also recommends that women be hormone free at least one week (five to seven days) per month. Otherwise, we risk reducing sensitivity at the hormone receptor sites. In perimenopausal, menopausal, and postmenopausal women, this protocol is recommended.[30] Many women find that they require a higher dose at different times of the month or even for the entire 21-day period each month.

Many registered compounding pharmacists work with physicians who prescribe natural hormones. Many physicians who prescribe bioidentical hormones are comfortable using natural estrogens somewhat routinely. Those physicians, who are more informed regarding the dangers of estrogens and estrogen dominance, seldom recommend anything except natural progesterone to women who are suffering hormonal imbalance during any of the life cycles.

The adrenal cortex (when functioning optimally) maintains our supply of estrogen and progesterone after the ovaries no longer perform that function. Estrogen is also stored in body fat and then metabolized by the liver. Progesterone should remain in adequate supply as well. A progesterone deficiency is not "normal," but it is common. The Lord did not design our bodies to run out of progesterone or estrogen during midlife. But in the industrialized world, an alarming number of women are deficient in progesterone.

Most women in the industrialized world now suffer from hormonal imbalance throughout each of the major life cycles— the childbearing years, perimenopause, menopause, and postmenopause. In contrast, most women in other parts of the world—the Pacific Rim, Africa, and South America:

1. Do not suffer from PMS (Premenstrual Syndrome).

2. Do not experience degenerative symptoms of menopause—hot flashes, night sweats, vaginal dryness, bloating, weight gain, mood swings, headaches.

3. Do not have the diseases that are now associated with postmenopause in the industrialized countries (osteoporosis, heart disease, and memory loss).

There are obvious bio-cultural differences between people in the industrialized world and people in the developing countries. We now know (according to the epidemiological studies) that there is a direct connection between dietary and lifestyle choices, and degenerative disease. The United States is the world leader in degenerative disease. Hormonal imbalance is only one of our many afflictions. Research is conclusive: The foods we choose to eat, and the exercises we choose to do, are major determinants of health.

Estrogen dominance is another key factor in degenerative disease. Xenobiotics are the petrochemical derivatives that mimic the hormones in our bodies (estrogens, progesterone, and others) and occupy the same receptors. We are inundated with them. These molecules contaminate our environment, our food chain, and the air that we breathe. We are ingesting xenobiotics when we consume beef and dairy that are not organic, because they contain high concentrations of herbicides and pesticides. Consequently, we become estrogen dominant.

Foreign hormones cause estrogen dominance in women, men, and children as well. If testing reveals that we have a progesterone deficiency, we can resolve the problem with natural

transdermal progesterone cream. I recommend the following
testing services for saliva hormone screening:

Aeron LifeCycles Laboratory: 1-800-631-7900

Body Balance: 1-888-891-3061
(a division of Great Smokies Diagnostic Laboratory)

For more information see Part Five: Vital Resources

According to David T. Zava, Ph.D., expert in biomedical
research, saliva is the best type of body fluid that we could use
to test hormonal levels. According to Dr. Zava, "Saliva reflects
the bioactive levels of endogenous hormones. It is more representative of what amount of hormone is biologically available to the target tissues of the body."[31]

Since few women actually require even small amounts of
bio-identical estrogens (once they have begun taking micronized progesterone), it is unwise to begin taking even a safe
estrogen (such as bio-identical estriol) until the natural progesterone has had time to impact the body. This could be
several weeks or several months. Progesterone, in the overwhelming majority of women, encourages the rise of estrogen,
testosterone, and corticosteroids to optimal levels.[32]

A compounding pharmacist has shared with me a variety
of protocols used by physicians with whom she works. My
own physician friends have contributed a great deal to my
understanding as well. Those with whom I speak most often
are cautious about prescribing estrogen (and, of course, would
only prescribe bio-identical estrogen). Many believe as I do
that by correcting deficiencies in progesterone, by adhering to
an optimal dietary regimen, and by supplementing our diets
with whole food concentrates and nutraceuticals, women have
the best possible hope for achieving hormonal balance and
optimal health.

Often women find relief from all symptoms of hormonal
imbalance simply by using progesterone twice a day. An optimal diet and specific nutritional supplements nourish the
adrenals. I recommend vitamin E (800 IU d-alphatocopherol,

dry capsules), selenium (60 mcg), grape seed extract (50 mg), pycnogenol (60 mg), red wine polyphenols (60 mg), coenzyme Q-10 (30 mg), and ginkgo biloba (120 mg). I also take vitamin C ascorbate, 2500 mg twice a day. I begin each day with at least a tablespoon of freshly ground flaxseed with my food and consume plant estrogens (either soy or freshly ground flaxseed) with every meal. Progesterone and a diet rich in plant estrogens, essential fatty acids, green leafy vegetables, and intact grains are keys to overcoming degenerative disease associated with hormonal imbalance. A complete discussion of this topic follows in Part Six.

Although I consume an optimal diet and drink organic whole food concentrates three times a day, I cover my nutritional bases with a multiple mineral supplement and a separate multiple vitamin supplement. No man, woman, or child can afford to miss any of the essential nutrients. The homocysteine connection with coronary artery disease underscores the importance of an adequate multiple vitamin supplement containing appropriate amounts of folate, B12, and B6.[33] These B vitamins are necessary for the prevention of birth defects as well. Of course, these isolated nutrients are hardly substitutes for the whole foods that I discuss in Part Six. We simply need to be certain that we consume all of the essential nutrients every day.

Bio-Identical Hormones

When we speak of natural hormones, we are talking about the structure of the molecule, not the source of the hormone. Bio-identical hormones have the same molecular structure as the hormones that our bodies produce.

Natural progesterone has the same molecular structure as the progesterone produced by the human body. Natural progesterone is not toxic. It is safe. Within a range of 25 mg twice a day to 100 mg twice a day, each woman must conscientiously determine the optimal dosage for herself. We need to rotate the sites where we apply the transdermal cream. Aeron LifeCycles verified the progesterone content of the cream I use through their product integrity certification program. I know exactly how much progesterone is contained in each ounce of cream, according to independent testing. I suggest that women *begin* with no more than 25 mg twice a day applied to the soft tissue inside the forearm, on the breasts, on the abdomen, or inside the thighs. Some women require more cream. However, time is required for hormonal balance. For some, the changes are almost overnight. For others, progress occurs slowly, and often in conjunction with dietary and lifestyle changes. The need for progesterone supplementation can be determined by saliva hormone testing. Testing can also be used to confirm that the progesterone cream is working. Most women are more interested in being symptom free than in looking at test results. I use a micronized cream that is absorbed rapidly. I know the product, and I know that I am getting a physiological dose each day. Here are some of the ways women use bio-identical hormones and achieve excellent results:

Directions for use:

Apply cream to appropriate sites (inside of the upper arm, upper thigh, breasts, or abdomen), rotating sites from one application to the next. Use the cream twice a day, twelve hours between each application.

Childbearing years:

Apply 25 mg twice daily on days 14 through 26 of cycle.

Perimenopause:

Apply 25 mg twice daily on days 8 through 20 of the menstrual cycle; then increase to 50 mg on days 21 through 28 of cycle. Do not use during days of menstruation. Even if menstruation does not begin on the 28th day of cycle, stop using the cream for seven days—beginning on the 29th day of the cycle.

Menopause, surgical menopause, or postmenopause:

Apply 25 mg to 50 mg twice daily. Use the cream for twenty-one days. Discontinue cream for seven days after each twenty-one day period of use.

PMS

Micronized progesterone cream, three weeks a month, 50 mg to 200 mg at least twice a day.

(Treating PMS may involve high doses of natural progesterone in order to overcome estrogen dominance. Treatment of PMS using high doses of progesterone requires a competent physician.)

Perimenopause or Menopause

Natural progesterone cream, three weeks a month, 25 mg to 200 mg at least twice a day.

If symptoms persist, many physicians and patients decide to add Tri-Estrogen (0.625 mg to 2.5 mg twice daily) to the protocol using natural progesterone cream (50 mg to 200 mg twice daily for three weeks out of the month). Estrogen, of course, requires a prescription—and a wise physician's advice and care.

Bi-Estrogen is also growing in popularity among many conscientious physicians. It is available in both the transdermal cream and in capsules.

Bi-Estrogen contains:

80% estriol	or	90% estriol
20% estradiol		10% estradiol

The usual dose of Bi-Estrogen is 0.625 mg to 2.5 mg twice daily.

Physicians who recommend bio-identical estrogen for those patients with unresolved issues (such as vaginal dryness) must consider the risks when prescribing even natural estrogens to those who have a history of cancer. For this reason, the Bi-Estrogen with 90 percent estriol formula gives patients both peace of mind and relief of symptoms.

Estriol cream applied vaginally is, perhaps, the safest way to use estrogen in dealing with vaginal dryness. The dosage frequently used is 0.3% estriol cream, inserted three times a week with a vaginal applicator. The patient would then be taking 3 mg per dose of estriol.

Surgical Menopause

Natural progesterone cream, three weeks a month,
50 mg to 200 mg twice daily.
Plus Tri-Estrogen 0.625 mg to 2.5 mg twice daily.

If the patient's testosterone remains low, even with high doses of progesterone, a physician might prescribe *natural testosterone* 0.25 mg to 0.5 mg daily. The physiological dose for women is 0.25 mg to 0.5 mg. Testosterone requires a prescription. Women should seek a competent physician if natural testosterone or natural estrogen is indicated.

[*EstraTest contains 2.5 mg methyltestosterone (5 to 10 times the physiological dose) plus synthetic estrogens. Even the half-strength EstraTest HS contains 1.25 mg methyltestosterone (much higher than the physiological dose). Side effects from using that dosage are irritability and aggressiveness. EstraTest is, of course, one of the worst possible choices.*]

Postmenopause

Natural progesterone, three weeks a month,
25 mg to 100 mg twice daily.

Some physicians cling to the notion that natural estrogen is needed at this stage of life. I would agree only if there were clear indications. If so, Tri-Estrogen and Bi-Estrogen are two possible choices. However, my personal choice would be estriol alone, because it is the safest estrogen to use. The time when estriol is most clearly indicated is when other protocols haven't relieved vaginal dryness and atrophy, a condition that sets women up for vaginitis and cystitis. Dietary and lifestyle factors impact our ability to regenerate. Estrogen, even bio-identical estrogen, ought to be a last resort. The 0.3% estriol cream inserted vaginally would be my personal choice.

Tri-Estrogen mimics the natural pattern of circulating estrogens:

10 to 20% estrone

10 to 20% estradiol

60 to 80% estriol

This formula, developed by Jonathan V. Wright, M.D., is conservative and popular. It is widely available in compounding pharmacies. The average dose is 2.5 mg. Many physicians who use only natural hormones prescribe Tri-Estrogen to all of their patients who have not had cancer.

[*Author's Note: Jonathan Wright, M.D., is one of the most outspoken critics of FDA policy. Insisting that vitamins, minerals and other nutrients are not drugs, but natural substances, he protests the FDA's jurisdiction over them. He is a real hero and one of the world's experts in nutritional biochemistry.*]

I would urge a relative or friend to first use natural estriol alone, if indeed estrogen were indicated, before using Bi-Estrogen or Tri-Estrogen. And by "indicated" I would mean if worrisome symptoms persisted after an optimal diet and a full course of whole food concentrates, nutritional supplements, and nutraceuticals had been followed for a long while. Most people simply do not understand the power of food. Soybeans alone are an ideal remedy for vaginal dryness and other symptoms of hormonal imbalance. This short statement by Neil Solomon, M.D., Ph.D., emphasizes the measurable ways in which naturally occurring substances in foods powerfully affect physiologic processes:

> Dr. Ingemar Joelsson, former Chairman and Professor of Gynecology in Sweden, found that postmenopausal women eating the equivalent of about ¾ cup of soybeans a day had increased estrogenic activity and decreased headaches, hot flashes and vaginal drying. It is well established that women who use soybeans as a major dietary component have less menopausal symptoms, and a decrease in hormone-related cancers such as breast and uterus cancers.[34]

Before considering bio-identical estrogen, I would certainly try black cohosh for a six-month period. Numerous studies indicate that black cohosh (*Cimicifuga racemosa*) relieves night sweats, hot flashes, and vaginal dryness. It is, perhaps, the most well-documented natural alternative to hormone replacement therapy. Most of the research comes from Germany. Many experts report long-term use with no side effects. Others recommend using black cohosh for three to six months and then discontinuing its use. The short-term side effects that have been reported are minor: dizziness, nausea, and diarrhea. Black cohosh has an incredible record for eliminating menopausal and perimenopausal symptoms: hot flashes, night sweats, insomnia, headaches, depression, and anxiety. An optimal diet is foundational. Phytoestrogens (isoflavones and lignans) are vital. (See Part Six.) Progesterone supplementation is essential for those whose levels are too low. The nutritional protocols mentioned above should then be included. If, after those issues are resolved, a woman still has symptoms of hormonal imbalance, black cohosh seems to me the best next step.

The first step is to lay the foundation for optimal health outlined in Part Six. An optimal diet, vigorous exercise, plenty of phytoestrogens (e.g., lignans from flaxseed and isoflavones from soybeans), the nutritional supplements outlined in this section, and natural progesterone are the best means of achieving hormonal balance and ending estrogen dominance.

Notes

1. Jerilynn C. Prior, M.D., "One Voice on Menopause," *JAMWA* 49, no. 1 (1994): 28.

2. Ibid., 27.

3. Ibid.

4. Ibid., 28.

5. A.T. Leather, M. Savras, and J.W. Studd, "Endometrial Histology and Bleeding Patterns after Eight Years of Continuous

Combined Estrogen and Progestin Therapy in Postmenopausal Women," *Obstetrics and Gynecology* 78 (1991): 1008-1010.

6. Prior, "One Voice on Menopause," 28.

7. Ibid.

8. Ibid.

9. Ibid.

10. John R. Lee, M.D., with David T. Zava, Ph.D. *The Secrets of Natural Hormone Therapy: Keys to Preventing Women's Most Serious Health Problems* (Harry DeLigter Productions, 1996), two audiocassettes.

11. Ibid.

12. Ibid.

13. Ibid.

14. Ibid.

15. Ibid.

16. Ibid.

17. Marcus Laux, N.D., and Christine Conrad, *Natural Woman, Natural Menopause* (New York: HarperCollins Publishers, 1997), 46.

18. John R. Lee, M.D., with Virginia Hopkins, *What your Doctor May Not Tell You about Menopause: The Breakthrough Book on Natural Progesterone* (New York: Warner Books, 1996), 92.

19. Lee, with Zava, *Natural Hormone Therapy*, audiocassettes.

20. Lee, with Hopkins, *What Your Doctor May Not Tell You*, 187.

21. Ibid.

22. Lee, *Natural Progesterone*, 25.

23. Lee, with Hopkins, *What Your Doctor May Not Tell You*, 40.

24. Ibid., 42.

25. *Los Angeles Times*, 24 March 1997.

26. Lee, with Zava, *Natural Hormone Therapy*, audiocassettes.

27. Ibid.

28. Ibid.

29. Ibid.

30. Lee, *Natural Progesterone,* 80.

31. Lee, with Zava, *Natural Hormone Therapy,* audiocassettes.

32. Lee, *Natural Progesterone,* 13.

33. Karl Dalery, M.D.; Suzanne Lussier-Cacan, Ph.D.; Jacob Selhub, Ph.D.; et al., "Homocysteine and Coronary Artery Disease in French Canadian Subjects: Relation with Vitamins B12, B6, Pyridoxal Phosphate, and Folate," *American Journal of Cardiology* 75, no. 16 (1995): 1107-1111;

Eric B. Rimm, Sc.D.; Walter C. Willett, M.D., Dr. P.H.; Frank B. Hu, M.D., Ph.D.; et al., "Folate and Vitamin B6 from Diet and Supplements in Relation to Risk of Coronary Heart Disease among Women," *Journal of the American Medical Association* 279, no. 5 (1998): 359-364;

Petra Verhoef; Frans J. Kok; Dick A.C.M. Kruyssen; et al, "Plasma Total Homocysteine, B Vitamins, and Risk of Coronary Athero-sclerosis," *Arteriosclerosis, Thrombosis and Vascular Biology* 17, no. 5 (1997): 989-995.

34. Neil Solomon, M.D., Ph.D., "Natural Strategies Can Substitute for Hormone Replacement Therapy (HRT)," *The Experts' Optimal Health Journal,* vol. 1, issue 2 (1997), 11.

————————————————————————— Part Four

Who Is Pushing
Synthetic Estrogen and Horse Estrogen?

Exposing the Deception

Anyone who is clearly attending to the research and who is pursuing safe, efficacious answers to hormonal imbalance must surely come to the conclusion that it is unwise to use:

1. estrogens that are not identical to those produced by the body,
2. conjugated (mixed) estrogens (e.g., Premarin), or
3. naturally circulating estrogens that do not mimic the pattern of naturally circulating estrogens in the human body (e.g., using estradiol, estrone, and estriol in proportions which are *not* physiologic).

Why? Research clearly indicates that these actions pose health risks and are life threatening.

There are many choices to make in overcoming hormonal imbalance, but the truth is this: conventional estrogen replacement therapy (ERT) and conventional hormone replacement therapy (HRT) are unthinkable options for those of us who understand and acknowledge the full range of safe and effective options available. The driving force behind these drugs is the marketing power of the pharmaceutical industry. The enormous financial success of ERT and HRT continues to fuel the propaganda machine. But as more and more of us write and talk about the issue of hormonal imbalance and present the research exposing the dangers of patentable hormones, the sooner consumers will begin demanding easier access to safe and efficacious natural hormones.

Therapies That Are Neither Optimal nor Appropriate

An example of an artificial estrogen is ethinyl estradiol that is altered from the natural estrogen. Thus, it qualifies as a patentable product, and the manufacturer has an exclusive right to sell it. Ethinyl estradiol is not an improvement over natural estradiol. In fact, the new molecular structure is different from any estrogen ever found in nature. It is commonly used in estrogen supplements and contraceptives, even though its high oral absorption and slow metabolism and elimination put consumers at risk.

Dr. John R. Lee talks about the problems we encounter when using synthetic compounds instead of natural steroids. Because atoms have been added to these compounds at unusual positions, their molecular shapes have been changed. Consequently, synthetic steroids are not subject to the usual metabolic control provided by our enzymes:

1. The effects of these steroids cannot be "tuned down" or "turned off."
2. Nor can these synthetic compounds be efficiently excreted by the body's usual enzymatic mechanisms.[1]

Next, we should carefully examine Premarin, the most widely prescribed drug in America and perhaps the most bizarre in terms of the number of women willing to consume it. Premarin contains horse estrogen that has been extracted from pregnant mares' urine. Premarin contains 48 percent estrone, according to some sources, or 75 to 80 percent, according to others. In either case, the percentage of estrone is too high. In the human body, estrone is in balance with estradiol and estriol.

The first problem is that the amount of estrone in Premarin is out of balance. The second problem is that estrone converts to estradiol in the body; estradiol is the circulating estrogen that increases the risk of cancer. The natural pattern for circulating estrogens in the body is quite different from Premarin. The pattern for naturally circulating estrogens is:

10 to 20% estrone
10 to 20% estradiol
60 to 80% estriol

The third problem is that Premarin also contains equilin and equilenin (horse estrogens), as well as synthetic additives.

Why are the proponents of natural hormone therapy concerned about Premarin? There are several reasons, all based on the problems just mentioned. The 48 percent (or higher) estrone content in the formula is too high, according to those researchers who regard the natural pattern for circulating hormones in the human body as the appropriate standard. Estrone itself is a problem because it converts to estradiol, which has been implicated as the circulating estrogen that increases the risk of cancer. The foreign estrogenic elements (horse estrogens) are wildly unnatural. Even though they may perform as human estrogens do in the body, they are potentially cancer producing. And finally, the synthetic additives pose an additional health risk.

> Recent media attention focused on reports of an increased risk of breast cancer in women in the Nurses Health Study who had been on estrogen longer than 5 years. What was never addressed by any of the physicians or health writers commenting on this disturbing information is that the overwhelming majority of women in the series were taking the conjugated equine estrogens, not 17-beta estradiol.
>
> With what we know about (1) how long the equine estrogens stay in the human body (anywhere from 8-14 weeks after the last dose), and (2) the stronger "attachment strength" (affinity) of the equine estrogens for the body estradiol receptors (especially the breasts, where estrogens may concentrate in the fat tissue), it seems incredible to me that *no one is talking about* a possible

link between accumulations of equine estrogens in breast
tissue and the observed higher risk of breast cancer with
long-term use . . .

Even in 1995, with other options available for a number
of years, conjugated equine estrogens (usually Premarin)
*account for about 85 percent of all estrogen prescriptions in
the U.S.*[2]

The word estrogen is actually misleading. The word estrogen refers to a class of hormones with estrous activity. The three most important hormones in the estrogen class are estrone (E1), estradiol (E2), and estriol (E3). When estrogen is dominant, it can cause breast stimulation resulting in breast fibrocysts and/or cancer. "Among the three major natural estrogens, estradiol is the most stimulating to breast tissue, estrone is second, and estriol by far the least."[3] And of course, estrone converts to estradiol. Estriol is perhaps noncarcinogenic and may actually be anticarcinogenic.[4]

But what is the great debate about? Why must women agonize over the decision to use ERT or HRT? The answer is money—and lots of it. Premarin has been among the most frequently prescribed drugs for over two decades. In spite of all the deaths and all the dangers, physicians continue to prescribe a variety of hormones that are patented and marketed aggressively by the pharmaceutical industry.

Unopposed Estrogen

Studies from the 1970s revealed that when estrogen is given alone (known as unopposed estrogen), without a progestin or progesterone, it carries with it a high risk of endometrial cancer and possibly other cancers, including breast cancer. Through a landmark journal article published in 1975, the news got out that women on ERT had a 7.6 times greater risk of cancer. Premarin was the most commonly prescribed estrogen at that time, just as it is now. Over six million women were using Premarin in 1975. We do not know how many women died as a result of the high dosages of Premarin used in the 1960s and 1970s; we simply know that many did.

Patients who have been advised by their physicians to take unopposed estrogen (and amazingly enough, many women continue to be ill advised) need to get a copy of this journal article.[5] I suggest they give a copy to their physician and ask what he or she has in mind.

Another landmark study that all women need to consider is the Postmenopausal Estrogen/Progestin Interventions (PEPI) Trial. Almost as interesting as the trial itself is the way in which various institutions, journalists, and health professionals regard the various findings. If readers can grasp the ways in which government institutions, medical professionals, and journalists serve business interests, they will be better able to protect themselves from unenlightened physicians.

Description of the PEPI Trial

The PEPI Trial is the first major clinical trial to examine the effects of sex hormones on heart disease risk factors in postmenopausal women. Scientists, whose support came from the National Heart, Lung, and Blood Institute (NHLBI), tested the effects of estrogen replacement therapy on the following factors which affect a woman's risk of heart disease:

1. HDL-Cholesterol
2. Systolic Blood Pressure
3. Fibrinogen (a blood clotting factor predictive of stroke and heart attack)
4. Insulin

The National Heart, Lung, and Blood Institute (NHLBI) administered and primarily funded the trial. Four other institutes of the National Institutes of Health provided co-funding for the PEPI study: the National Institute of Child Health and Human Development, the National Institute of Arthritis and Musculoskeletal and Skin Diseases, the National Institute of Diabetes and Digestive and Kidney Diseases, and the National Institute on Aging.

Nearly 900 women (875 to be exact) ages forty-five to sixty-four from seven clinical centers across the United States participated in the study. Thirty-two percent of the women had previously had a hysterectomy. The administrators of the study randomly assigned each of the women to one of the following five treatment groups; each of the treatment groups following a different regimen:

1. Placebo Use (Using an Inactive Substance)
2. Daily Estrogen Use
3. Daily Estrogen Plus a Synthetic Progestin Taken Daily for Twelve Days per Month
4. Daily Estrogen Plus Daily Synthetic Progestin
5. Daily Estrogen Plus a Natural (Micronized) Progesterone (MP) Taken Daily for Twelve Days per Month

Groups 3 and 4 listed above used synthetic progestins. These progestins have numerous risks and produce many side effects, as we will discuss later in this chapter. The natural (micronized) progesterone used by group number 5 listed above is produced by chemical conversion and is identical in every way to the progesterone hormone produced in our bodies. Natural progesterone is a bio-identical hormone absolutely indistinguishable from the hormone produced in our bodies.

I will discuss three points of view regarding the PEPI Trial. First, I will examine the summary of the PEPI Trial presented in a report from the government institution that funded the study (the National Heart, Lung, and Blood Institute). Second, I will share some of the comments on the PEPI Trial made by the *New York Times* medical writer, Jane E. Brody. And third, I will share my own point of view interspersed throughout the entire discussion of the PEPI Trial. Each of these views helps us to understand why consumers are confused about hormone therapy. Safe and efficacious solutions are constantly obscured by well-financed studies that serve business interests.

The NHLBI description of the PEPI Trial was released to the press in a four-page report on their letterhead. The report is entitled "The Postmenopausal Estrogen/Progestin Interventions (PEPI) Trial."[6]

This is my summary of key topics in the order in which they were presented by NHLBI:

1. Each of the four hormonal regimens tested produced significant increases in the levels of HDL (good cholesterol).

2. The most favorable increases in the HDL levels occurred in those individuals taking either estrogen alone or estrogen combined with micronized (natural) progesterone.

3. The other two estrogen/progestin combinations produced significantly greater increases in HDL cholesterol levels than the placebo group (those using an inactive substance).

4. Neither the estrogen/progestin combinations nor the estrogen/natural progesterone combination tested in the PEPI Trial caused hyperplasia (cell growth in the uterine lining). Hyperplasia is a potentially harmful condition that sometimes develops into cancer. However, estrogen taken alone significantly increased the occurrence of severe hyperplasia in women with a uterus.

[*Note from Dr. Dorian: The writer of this report referred to the three hormone therapies in point number 4 as "the three estrogen/progestin combinations" as though there were no significant difference between synthetic progesterone (progestins) and natural progesterone. And yet, the differences could hardly be exaggerated. Progestins cause numerous side effects and pose significant health risks. Natural progesterone has no known side effects and an amazingly wide range of benefits.*]

[*Note from "A Natural Approach to Menopause" by Neal Barnard, M.D. (President of the Physicians Committee for Responsible Medicine): "Altered forms of progesterone, called progestins (e.g. Provera), are heavily promoted by drug companies and are commonly prescribed by doctors. But these unnatural chemicals do not quite fit into the body's systems for using and eliminating progesterone. They are the biological equivalent of using the wrong replacement part in your car's engine. While the pharmaceutical companies' financial machinery hums along just fine, your biological machinery can have a multitude of side effects, ranging from facial hair growth and depression to heart disease, liver problems, and even breast cancer. The body was built to use natural progesterone, not inexact copies."*][7]

5. A quote from NHLBI director, Dr. Claude Lenfant: "The results of this landmark study provide the best available

guide for postmenopausal women and their physicians, as they seek safe hormonal regimens that will improve their heart disease risk factors." The next sentence of the letter stated that heart disease is the number one killer of American women and that each year 250,000 women die of the disease.[8]

Another quote from Dr. Lenfant: "We must wait for the results of large clinical trials such as the Women's Health Initiative to determine whether increasing HDL ultimately reduces a woman's chance of developing or dying from heart disease. Until then, the PEPI results are a significant step forward in our understanding of hormone therapy."[9]

[*Note from Dr. Dorian: The big marketing push for HRT is the supposed benefit for the heart. And yet, no one knows whether or not increasing HDL will prevent anyone from dying of heart disease. There are other factors that cause heart disease. What we do know is what is written on the Provera package insert: "The following adverse reactions have been observed in patients receiving estrogen-progestin combination drugs: rise in blood pressure in susceptible individuals, premenstrual-like syndrome, changes in libido, changes in appetite, cystitis-like syndrome, fatigue, headache, loss of scalp hair, erythema multiforme, erythema nodosum, hemorrhagic eruption, itching, dizziness, nervousness, backache. In view of these observations, patients on progestin therapy should be carefully observed."*][10]

6. All of the treatments except the placebo caused significant decreases in LDL-cholesterol and fibrinogen. Neither unopposed estrogen nor "estrogen/progestin" combinations increased blood pressure as had been previously believed. Notice that the writer uses "estrogen/progestin" to also mean estrogen/natural progesterone—as though they were one and the same. This is a mistake many physicians make; their ignorance regarding the risk-free benefits of natural progesterone is appalling.

7. Then, in a most casual tone, buried on page three came this bit of information: "The PEPI investigators reported that one-third of the women with a uterus assigned to unopposed

estrogen developed severe endometrial changes, diagnosed as adenomatous or atypical hyperplasias. These conditions are potentially precancerous."[11]

By the third year of this study, over 50 percent of the women with a uterus taking unopposed estrogen had to drop out because of their endometrial changes. That, of course, was part of the PEPI protocol. They had decided in advance not to totally finish off those women taking unopposed estrogen just to prove a point. The paragraph following that important news item is a quote by Elizabeth Barrett-Connor, M.D., professor and chair, Department of Family and Preventive Medicine, University of California, San Diego, and PEPI Steering Committee chair:

> These results provide the strongest evidence to date that estrogen given alone produces the best effect on HDL-cholesterol. However, the high rate of potentially harmful endometrial changes makes combination hormone therapy advisable for most women with a uterus.[12]

What does she mean by "the high rate of potentially harmful endometrial changes makes combination hormone therapy advisable for most women with a uterus?" Why would anyone recommend unopposed estrogen for any woman with or without a uterus? Why do so many physicians continue to do so?

[Another note from "Approach to Menopause" by Neal Barnard, M.D.: "The doctor writes out a prescription for estrogen pills or patches, saying they will replace the hormones her body ought to be making . . . The doctor acknowledges that there is an increased risk of uterine and breast cancer, but argues that the benefits to the heart and bones are worth taking the chance. Other risks enter into the discussion: strokes, blood clots, and water retention, among others. Women . . . may have menopausal symptoms, and they would like a solution. But they are looking for something safe that doesn't cause more problems than it solves."][13]

8. Finally, the fibrinogen levels of the PEPI participants on active treatment did not rise as it did in the placebo group. Here is Dr. Barrett-Connor's comment on that finding:

This is the most convincing evidence so far that hormone replacement may prevent the rise in fibrinogen that occurs with age. The Framingham Heart Study found that the women with high fibrinogen levels had twice the risk of heart disease as women with low fibrinogen.[14]

[*Dorian note: The major point of the Framingham Heart Study is that in over thirty-five years of the study no one has had a heart attack whose blood cholesterol has been under 150. Dietary and lifestyle changes prevent and cure a wide range of degenerative diseases. Why would anyone want to take life-threatening drugs in order to increase the chance of not getting a heart attack? There are sure ways to prevent and cure heart attacks while achieving optimal health. What is there to celebrate in the PEPI Trial? Not all of the medical professionals are fooled.*]

[*Another comment by Neal Barnard, M.D.: "Take heart: There are dietary steps, other lifestyle changes, and natural hormone preparations that can make menopause much more manageable. They are better for your heart and bones than estrogen prescriptions could ever hope to be, and they accomplish these things without the side effects of estrogens."*][15]

Jane Brody, medical writer for the *New York Times*, represents the medical industrial establishment in her evaluation of the PEPI Trial. She assumes that estrogen is a tried and true measure for the prevention of heart disease:

> It had been established that estrogen alone, while highly effective against cardiovascular problems, causes an increase in uterine cancer.[16]

Then she sets us up for what we are to believe is a great breakthrough. According to Brody, the reassuring news to postmenopausal women is this:

> A combination of the two hormones [estrogen and progestin] can help prevent uterine cancer while not significantly reducing the cardiovascular benefits associated with using estrogen alone as a hormone replacement.[17]

What Brody doesn't know or report is that "when the synthetic progestins are added to HRT the breast cancer rates go up after 4 or 5 years. You also get all of the other side effects of the progestins."[18]

The most telling, and chilling, paragraph concludes her coverage of the PEPI Trial.

> A future report from the study will describe the effects of the various hormone regimens on the women's bones. Estrogen replacement is known to greatly reduce the accelerated bone loss that typically occurs in the early postmenopausal years, but the effects on bone loss of various progestin regimens has not been thoroughly studied.[19]

Here is what John R. Lee learned from his patients during fifteen years of clinical practice: osteoporosis is due to (1) excessive bone loss, (2) not enough new bone formation, or (3) both. When patients are osteoclast dominant, they are absorbing away old bone (estrogen slightly restrains the osteoclast function); when patients are deficient in osteoblast function, they cannot rebuild bone. With or without estrogen, Dr. Lee watched patient after patient rebuild bone by using natural progesterone cream. He included regular bone mineral density tests as a routine part of the patients' evaluations.[20]

As I mentioned in Part Three, he also found that estrogen helped patients remain stable, but did not reverse bone lost. Those patients not on hormones had a 4½ percent bone loss in three years, patients on estrogen remained the same during the three year period; patients on natural progesterone gained 15 percent more bone during the three year period.[21]

Why isn't this reported widely and constantly as a public service for the elderly? There's no money to be made by the pharmaceutical industry. All of us need to be involved in getting the news out.

> The problems that women are most hampered by— osteoporosis, breast cancer, decline in mental acuity, loss of libido—these are related to progesterone. They are not estrogen problems.[22]

The pharmaceutical industry provides and sponsors speakers for the continuing medical education of physicians. The pharmaceutical industry does not fund studies documenting the efficacy of natural healing therapies. Rather, they seek to support efficacy and safety of their patent medicines. Where are the patients' rights to appropriate medical care in all of this? They are lost in the commerce of practicing medicine.

> Few people know that the definition of malpractice hinges on whether or not the practice is common among one's medical peers, and has little (usually nothing) to do with whether the practice is beneficial or not. A doctor willing to study, to learn the ins and outs of an alternative medical therapy, and to put what he has learned into practice in helping patients is potentially exposing himself to serious charges of malpractice. And he can expect no help from organized medicine. Truth be known, medicine today is very disorganized and what passes as "organized medicine" is merely a handmaiden to the powers of health agencies and the pharmaceutical industry.[23]

When I talk to women who are afraid to continue ERT and HRT, I find that most of them never wanted to read the package insert before they began taking the medication. They tell me that they did not want to read the information, because they believed it would make them even more fearful. And yet, they took the drugs in spite of their fears, because a physician advised it. Most women do not have peace about ERT and HRT. Still, they find it hard to believe that there are safe and effective natural hormone therapies that offer solutions without creating problems. Why? Because their physician would surely know what is available, and he/she would recommend the very best products available. It is horrifying, given the influence that medical doctors have, that most physicians do not know how to help women and men achieve hormone balance naturally. Many simply don't understand the choices available. Others will not take a stand against the industry that produces synthetic hormones and patented hormones (e.g.,

Premarin), which pose health risks, for fear of losing favor with their peers. Some physicians seek alternatives for those who are nearest and dearest to them (their wives, mothers, and daughters), and yet, continue to push the patent medicines on their patients. As consumers continue to educate themselves, an army is in the making. Physicians who meet the genuine needs of their patients, and offer them the very best care possible, are in demand.

Sources of Confusion

The quote by *Newsday* on the top of *Dr. Susan Love's Hormone Book* reads: "The bible for a whole generation of menopausal women." The back cover includes these endorsements:

> Extraordinarily helpful . . . Thankfully, we've now got Love to interpret the medical fine print.
> - *Mirabella*

> One of the Best Books of 1997.
> - *Publishers Weekly*

> One of the ten most important women in medicine.
> - *Ladies' Home Journal*[24]

Misleading information abounds in this book, with no clear guidelines for optimally safe choices. Dr. Love's comments on micronized progesterone hardly lead the reader to believe that the product would be efficacious—

> In one randomized controlled double-blind study, micronized progesterone had fewer side effects, and a better effect on lipids and the endometrium, than a progestin. [She cites the writing group for the PEPI trial as her source.] But as clinicians or consumers, we're stuck with a nonstandardized product or possibly inferior standardized product because it's considered unprofitable to find out which is best for women. It is for this reason that progestins are still more commonly used.[25]

On page 272, she talks about the problem in finding a "skin cream" which contains a meaningful amount of progesterone. On the next page is a reprint of a 1996 Aeron LifeCycles list of products tested for progesterone content (with a toll-free number in small print at the bottom). She offers no information on the staggering success of transdermal progesterone creams and does not point out to readers that they may wish to contact Aeron LifeCycles directly to find a cream that contains sufficient progesterone. Instead she says:

> The skin creams have become somewhat controversial lately. There are a number of them on the market, claiming to contain progesterone and to decrease hot flashes and increase bone. Many of these actually have very little progesterone. The assumption is that because they are made from wild yam, they'll have the same effect as progesterone, which is also made from wild yam. Don't count on it.[26]

Finding a transdermal progesterone cream with sufficient natural progesterone is a simple procedure. Aeron LifeCycles Laboratory launched a new Product Integrity Certification Program (PIC) in February 1998 for the testing and certification of over-the-counter progesterone cream products. Clinicians and consumers are not "stuck with a nonstandardized product or a possibly inferior standardized product" as Dr. Love suggests. Many consumers and physicians have been using reliable creams for years, as a result of the grassroots information network that has existed for over two decades. Now, with the PIC Program, many more consumers will be able to find reliable products and escape the horrors of progestin.

Aeron LifeCycles Product Integrity Certification,
1-800-631-7900

On page 135, Dr. Love refers to progestins and progesterone as though they were essentially the same:

> I think we need more data about progestins and progesterone before we get carried away. But most of the medical community has taken a different approach to progestins and progesterone, an approach characterized by tunnel vision: it is simply assumed that the drugs protect the uterus and have no other effects. This is

unlikely to be the case with any hormone. In fact, many of the symptoms of perimenopause and menopause become worse when you take progestins and progesterone.[27]

On page 272, Dr. Love acknowledges that there is a difference between progesterone and progestin without explaining that it is a significant difference. People need to be warned about progestins. Progesterone has no known adverse side effects. Here are her words:

> Although natural progesterone—the form most like the hormone we produce naturally—is available, it's rarely used. It's plant-based and generic (like estriol), so it can't be patented . . . manufacturers can't make as much money from producing it and have less incentive to study it. Therefore, progestins, which are molecules that have been changed a bit and can therefore be patented, are more commonly prescribed. The terms, *progesterone* and *progestin,* are often used interchangeably, but they shouldn't be, since the actions of progesterone and progestin can be very different.[28]

Notice her choice of words—"the actions of progesterone and progestin can be very different." Here are three possible meanings of her use of the word "can":

1. progesterone and progestin *are able* to be very different
2. progesterone and progestin *are potentially capable* of being very different
3. progesterone and progestin *are permitted* to be very different

None of these usages are appropriate. Progesterone and progestins are significantly different, and the consequence of choosing one over the other could change the course of one's life.

In the spring of 1994, *Good Health* magazine, a publication of the Physicians Committee for Responsible Medicine, published an interview with John R. Lee, M.D., by Neal D. Barnard, M.D., president of the Physicians Committee for Responsible Medicine. Dr. Lee clearly explains the difference between progesterone and progestins:

Progesterone is not the same as progestin. Progesterone is a natural compound, so drug companies cannot patent it. To make a patentable medication, drug companies have to chemically alter it to make it unique. The result is progestins such as Provera. Unfortunately, the chemical alterations result in so many side effects that I caution against the use of progestins. If you look in the *Physicians' Desk Reference,* you see warnings about breast cancer, facial hair growth, depression, cardiovascular disease, liver disorders, and other problems which turn out to be very common.

Dr. Love keeps one foot in the alternative medicine camp by insisting that hormones are best used for the treatment of symptoms, and not for the prevention of disease. She also spends a great deal of time telling readers about her own very good lifestyle choices. She recognizes that there are benefits to exercise, phytoestrogens, and a plant-based diet. I regard this particular book as a real stumbling block for those women who want to understand why the transitional periods of life—perimenopause, menopause, and postmenopause—become nightmares. This book doesn't confront the real issues facing men, women, and children in the industrialized countries who are struggling with hormonal imbalance. The problems are comprehensible, and the solutions are clear. The steps to optimal health and fitness do not involve life-threatening drugs.

In chapter 1 of the book, *Natural Woman, Natural Menopause,* by Marcus Laux, N.D., and Christine Conrad, the authors talk about the false dilemma presented by mainstream physicians. The great deception is the notion that in order to get relief from symptoms, one must risk experiencing both the side effects and the long-term risks of HRT.

> At a recent symposium in Los Angeles, a well-known woman M.D. cancer specialist told the women in the audience, "There is no free lunch. If you want the benefits [of hormone therapy], you have to pay the price."[29]

The endnotes for the chapter reveal that the authors are quoting panelist Dr. Susan Love at "Women and Doctors," a

UCLA symposium held in May 1994. The key point of the book by Laux and Conrad is that bio-identical hormones offer help without the horrors of conventional hormone replacement therapy.

At the other end of the conventional medical spectrum, there are an incredible number of physicians such as Marianne Legato, M.D., with impressive credentials, who think that only one in five women does *not* need HRT and who highly recommend HRT for osteoporosis and cardiovascular benefits. Dr. Legato is sixty-two years old, an internist-cardiologist and director of the Partnership for Women's Health at Columbia University College of Physicians and Surgeons, and co-author of *The Female Heart* (Simon & Schuster, 1991). She has come to this amazing conclusion: "In terms of absolute contraindications for HRT, there are very few." She has also found justification for recommending Premarin: "I often prescribe Premarin because we have the most data about that compound. However, there are many ingredients in Premarin, and it is unclear what agent or agents are actually producing the beneficial effects."

The logic of this is amazing. The pharmaceutical industry has billions to spend on research studies. They spend their money on studies using patentable, and often unsafe, products. Does it then follow that we should use their unsafe, patentable products because there is more data on them than there is on the safe, natural, and efficacious products? Of course, it does not. But this is the kind of leap we make when we abandon the liberal arts in favor of highly specialized education. If we don't consider it our job to grapple with ideas outside of our specific fields of expertise, we lose part of what it is to be fully human. Since life itself is an interdisciplinary project, this approach leads to a kind of madness and self-imprisonment.

Many physicians, who present themselves as people open to alternative therapies and to complementary medicine, continue to support conventional hormone therapy, and the use of synthetic hormones and horse estrogens. Susan Lark, M.D., is described in a Keats Good Health Guide (*Making the Estrogen Decision: All the Information You Need to Make It—Including the*

Full Range of Natural Alternatives) as a noted authority on
women's health care and preventive medicine. The Keats guide
is taken from her book, *The Estrogen Decision*. Her comments
on Premarin:

> The most commonly prescribed estrogen tablet is
> Premarin, a conjugated equine estrogen derived from a
> pregnant mare's urine. It has been available since 1941,
> and much of the medical research has been done using
> this product. As a result, the benefits and side effects of
> Premarin are very well understood. Another benefit of
> Premarin is that it comes in a wider variety of doses
> than any of the other estrogen products. This allows for
> much more flexibility in determining the optimal treat-
> ment dosage for each woman user.[30]

The last statement is an amazing one. Imagine the fact
that it comes in a wide variety of doses as a legitimate reason
for using Premarin. All bio-identical estrogens—estrone, estradiol and estriol—are available in any dose the physician
requires, through a compounding pharmacy.

Like Dr. Love, Dr. Lark also fails to properly distinguish
progesterone from progestin:

> Women using progesterone therapy may suffer a num-
> ber of uncomfortable side effects. This is particularly
> true for women using the commonly prescribed pro-
> gestins, the synthetic forms of progesterone such as
> Provera. The side effects include the following: depres-
> sion and mood changes, breast tenderness and enlarge-
> ment, increased appetite, and headaches.[31]

The first sentence in the quote is simply wrong. She is
using the word progesterone to mean both natural and synthetic progesterone. There are no known side effects with
natural progesterone. The second sentence begins, "This is
particularly true for women using commonly prescribed progestins." Using "particularly" in this way can mean "only" or
"solely," but it can also mean "principally" or "mainly." No-
where is the outstanding role of natural progesterone explained.

Among those people who recommend only bio-identical hormones is a very wide range of recommendations. John R. Lee, M.D., is considered the foremost authority on the clinical uses of progesterone. An outline summary of his views are perhaps the best conclusion for this section:

1. Progesterone deficiencies exist and the problem is widespread.
2. Estrogen deficiency is largely a myth.
3. The problems which women in industrialized countries face are largely due to estrogen dominance.
4. Osteoporosis, breast cancer, decline in mental acuity, loss of libido—these are related to progesterone. They are not estrogen problems.
5. "I'm not against estrogen; if a woman needs a little estrogen for hot flashes or vaginal dryness, she can have some—but the typical woman won't need it."[32]

Notes

1. John R. Lee, M.D., *Natural Progesterone: The Multiple Roles of a Remarkable Hormone*, Revised ed. (Sebastopol, CA: BLL Publishing, 1993, 1997), 25.

2. Elizabeth Lee Vliet, M.D., *Screaming to Be Heard: Hormonal Connections Women Suspect . . . and Doctors Ignore* (New York: M. Evans and Company, 1995), 107.

3. Lee, *Natural Progesterone*, 73.

4. Alvin H. Follinstad, M.D., "Estriol, the Forgotten Estrogen," *Journal of the American Medical Association* 239, no. 1 (1978): 30.

5. H.K. Ziel, and W.D. Finkle, "Increased Risk of Endometrial Carcinoma among Users of Conjugated Estrogens," *New England Journal of Medicine* 293, no. 23 (1975): 1167-1170.

6. National Heart, Lung, and Blood Institute, "The Postmenopausal Estrogen/Progestin Interventions (PEPI) Trial" (Bethesda, MD: National Heart, Lung, and Blood Institute; National Institutes of Health; Public Health Service; U.S. Department of Health and Human Services), release, 17 November 1994. (Information

Office Telephone: 301-496-4236; Fax: 301-496-2405; 9000 Rockville Pike, Building 31, Room 4A-21 Bethesda, MD 20892).

7. Neal D. Barnard, M.D., "A Natural Approach to Menopause," Breast Cancer Prevention and Survival Series (Washington, DC: Physicians Committee for Responsible Medicine), p. 4, condensed from *Eat Right, Live Longer* (New York: Harmony Books, 1995).

8. NHLBI, PEPI Trial press release, 1.

9. Ibid., 2-3.

10. Provera brand of medroxyprogesterone acetate tablets, USP (Kalamazoo, MI: The Upjohn Company; repacked by Drug Distributors, Inc., Bluffton, IN) package insert.

11. NHLBI, PEPI Trial press release, 3.

12. Ibid.

13. Barnard, "Approach to Menopause," 1.

14. NHLBI, PEPI Trial press release, 3.

15. Barnard, "Approach to Menopause," 1.

16. Jane Brody, "New Therapy for Menopause Reduces Risks," *New York Times National*, 18 November 1994.

17. Ibid.

18. John R. Lee, M.D., with David T. Zava, Ph.D., *The Secrets of Natural Hormone Therapy: Keys to Preventing Women's Most Serious Health Problems* (Harry DeLigter Productions, 1996), two audiocassettes.

19. Brody, "New Therapy for Menopause."

20. Lee, with Zava, *Natural Hormone Therapy*, audiocassettes.

21. Ibid.

22. Ibid.

23. Lee, *Natural Progesterone*, 89.

24. Susan M. Love, M.D., with Karen Lindsey, *Dr. Susan Love's Hormone Book: Making Informed Decisions about Menopause* (New York: Random House, Times Books, 1998), back cover.

25. Ibid., 275.

26. Ibid., 272.

27. Ibid., 135.

28. Ibid., 272.

29. Marcus Laux, N.D., and Christine Conrad, *Natural Woman, Natural Menopause* (New York: HarperCollins Publishers, 1997), 6.

30. Susan M. Lark, M.D., *Making the Estrogen Decision: All the Information You Need to Make It—Including the Full Range of Natural Alternatives* (New Canaan, CT: Keats Publishing, 1996), 15.

31. Ibid., 35.

32. Lee, with Zava, *Natural Hormone Therapy*, audiocassettes.

Author's List of Vital Resources

Guidelines for Optimal Dietary Regimens

Oldways Preservation & Exchange Trust
25 First Street
Cambridge, MA 02141
617-621-3000
"Preserving traditions and fostering cultural exchange in the fields of food, cooking and agriculture"

Stated objectives of Oldways:

Slow the world-wide epidemic of preventable chronic diseases by encouraging healthier eating, drinking, exercise and lifestyle patterns.

Help to reduce pollution from agriculture (the largest source of surface water pollution) by discouraging chemically-intensive agriculture and promoting sustainable agriculture; and

Retard the steady loss of cultural and biological diversity by preserving traditional ways of growing, cooking and eating food.

—Oldways, page 1

What this author regards as one of the greatest contributions of Oldways:

Jointly with the Harvard School of Public Health, Oldways has published the "healthy eating" pyramids, three unique dietary guides based on worldwide dietary traditions closely associated with good health. One of these pyramids is based on Mediterranean diets, one on Asian diets, and one on Latin American diets.

The pyramids are alternatives to the outdated U.S. government's Food Guide Pyramid and offer highly palatable, healthful frameworks for dietary change. They also establish for the first time a scientific basis for the preservation and revitalization of traditional diets.

—Oldways, page 1

Physicians Committee for Responsible Medicine
5100 Wisconsin Avenue, NW
Suite 404
Washington, DC 20016
202 686-2210
Fax: 202 686-2216

"A coalition of 4000 physicians and 100,000 lay persons dedicated to making a difference in medical science and human health."

Stated accomplishments in the area of health and nutrition:

We introduced the New Four Food Groups and changed federal nutrition guidelines to include vegetarian diets for the first time.

We are working to educate people about cancer prevention through the Cancer Prevention and Survival Fund.

We are teaching children, their parents, and educators about healthful vegetarian diets through our school curriculum program.

—Letter to New PCRM Members

I join with PCRM in supporting "vigorous efforts for preventive medicine." Many of the PCRM publications are listed in the bibliography. All of them are worthwhile. Books by Neal D. Barnard, M.D., president of PCRM are also in the bibliography and are highly recommended.

Physicians Who Recommend Protocols Using Bio-Identical Hormones

American College for Advancement in Medicine (ACAM)
P.O. Box 3427
Laguna Hills, CA 92654

If you would like the name of an ACAM doctor near you, contact ACAM at: 1-800-532-3688

The American Association of
  Naturopathic Physicians (AANP)
601 Valley Street
Suite 105
Seattle, WA 98109
Telephone: 206-298-0126 (General Information)
206-298-0125 (Referral Service)

Saliva Hormone Test Kits

Aeron LifeCycles
1933 Davis Street, Ste. 310
San Leandro, CA 94577
Telephone: 1-800-631-7900
Fax: 510-729-0383

Body Balance
A Division of Great Smokies Diagnostic Laboratory
63 Zillicoa Street
Asheville, NC 28801-1074
Telephone: 1 000-891-3061
Fax: 1-828-253-4646

List of Certified Progesterone Creams

Aeron LifeCycles Product Integrity Certification Program

1. Aeron provides an objective, ongoing, scientific validation of the progesterone content of cream products sold over-the-counter to medical professionals and consumers. The list offers a simple way for health professionals and consumers to find products with verifiable amounts of progesterone.

2. The progesterone creams are tested by an independent HPLC laboratory and confirmed by RIA at Aeron.
3. Call Aeron LifeCycles toll-free (1-800-631-7900) and request a list. There is no charge for this service.

Consumer Action

American Preventive Medical Association (APMA)
P.O. Box 458
Great Falls, VA 22066
Telephone: 1-800-230-APMA

The Nutrition Action Health Letter
Center for Science in the Public Interest
1875 Connecticut Avenue Northwest
Suite 300
Washington, DC 20009-5728
Telephone: 202-332-9111

Excellent organization offering educational materials on health and nutrition.

Organic Whole Foods, Organic Whole Food Concentrates, and Nutritional Supplements

Marpé International
101 Bill Garland Road
Johnson City, Tennessee 37604
Telephone: 1-800-295-3477
Fax: 423-434-2333
www.marpeinternational.com

To Contact Terry Dorian, Ph.D.

Health Begins in Him Ministries
P.O. Box 458
Naples, NC 28760
www.healthbeginsinhim.org

—————————————————————— Part Six

Who Are the Healthiest People in the World?

- *What clinical and epidemiological studies tell us about the connection between dietary and lifestyle habits, and disease*
- *Protocols for overcoming irritable bowel disease and inflammatory bowel disease*
- *Optimal digestion and assimilation*
- *Protocols for managing diabetes (Type I), and for preventing and reversing diabetes (Type II)*

When we refer to optimal dietary regimens, we must discipline ourselves to consider the results of epidemiological studies. Such studies, which focus on the ways in which various diseases impact groups of people, give us vital information concerning the connection between dietary habits and degenerative disease. We can look at the studies and discover who the healthiest people in the world really are and why. As I have discussed in *Health Begins in Him* and in *The Cookbook Health Begins in Him*, the China-Cornell-Oxford Diet and Health Project established, among other things, that people who are genetically similar enjoy very different levels of health and wellness. The study also underscores the significant connection between dietary habits and disease. The rural Chinese are among the healthiest people in China and the world.[1]

Epidemiologists and nutritionists have studied the lifetime dietary habits of people living in Crete, much of the rest of Greece, and southern Italy. In the early 1960s, the adult life expectancy in this region "was among the highest in the world, and rates of coronary heart disease, certain cancers, and other diet-related chronic diseases were among the lowest in the world."[2] The life expectancy is especially significant in light of the limitations in existing medical services in the region at that time.

Epidemiological studies, conducted throughout the world, reveal that the healthiest people alive today have much in common. Their life-extending habits are simple for us to embrace, if we have the will to do so. These people consume an abundance of plant-based, minimally processed foods. For example, the rural Chinese eat an abundance of intact grain (i.e., grain before it is milled or flaked). Research reveals that many people living in primitive cultures consume very simple foods—grains, vegetables, beans, and little or no refined carbohydrates. In spite of the fact that they have relatively few food choices, their meals are festive, communal, and physically satisfying. Their cuisine is obviously strengthening as well. Men and women in these societies live vigorous mental and physical lives well beyond the age of ninety. In contrast, many Americans who have reached midlife begin seeking solutions to brain fog, short-term memory loss, and a wide range of life-threatening diseases. Our diets and lifestyles are costing us our lives!

We know that today, most of the people who live better and longer than we do are located in the Pacific Rim, in parts of Africa, and in South America. We also know that their dietary habits have these common characteristics.

1. They eat an abundance of plant-based foods, or they eat *only* plant-based foods.
2. They consume minimally processed, seasonally fresh, locally grown foods.
3. They consume little, or no, saturated fat.
4. They consume few, or no, sweets.
5. They eat an abundance of dietary fiber.

The research is conclusive. Food can heal our bodies. Plant-based regimens prevent and cure degenerative disease. Intact grains (e.g., wheat, barley, oats before they are milled or flaked) strengthen the body and help stabilize blood sugar levels; enzyme-rich raw vegetables and fruits nourish and revitalize the body; omega-3 and omega-6 essential fatty acids impact virtually every system in the body. Simple people, who have never studied health and nutrition, manage to achieve optimal health. We need to study and imitate their ways in order to prevent and reverse degenerative disease. But knowing lifetime dietary habits of the healthiest people in the world is just the beginning for those who want to achieve optimal health. Most of the people in western industrialized countries find themselves weakened and diseased after years, or lifetimes, of poor dietary choices. Often, allergies, food intolerances, and a wide range of diseases of the bowel prevent them from being able to digest and assimilate the foods they need most. They face a real challenge in getting the micronutrients and phytochemicals that are essential for optimal health. Often, such individuals must experience some healing before life-saving, high-fiber foods can even be tolerated.

Before getting into the specific, life-saving protocols for those suffering with diseases of the bowel, readers need to know the significant points of the China-Oxford-Cornell Diet and Health Project directed by T. Colin Campbell, Professor of Nutritional Biochemistry, Cornell University. Dr. Campbell considers this ongoing study to be one that will continue to generate relevant data for the next forty to fifty years.

The important findings of the China-Cornell-Oxford Diet and Health Project are:

1. The healthiest people in China get only 7 to 10 percent of their protein from animal sources (meat, fish, poultry, eggs, and dairy).
2. Those who are genetically predisposed place themselves at risk for disease when they consume even small amounts of animal protein.
3. A dietary regimen high in complex carbohydrates and low in fat (as opposed to a regimen high in refined carbohydrates, low in fiber, and high in fat) enables people to consume significantly more calories without gaining weight.

4. The Chinese do not suffer from iron deficiency while consuming plant-based regimens, nor do they suffer (as do many Americans) from iron overload.
5. The Chinese drastically reduce the likelihood of osteoporosis by avoiding foods that are high in phosphates (e.g., meat, poultry, fish, and dairy).

Much of this chapter focuses on the special challenges of those with irritable bowel disease and with diabetes (Type I and Type II). These topics concern everyone. Why? The number of people experiencing symptoms of irritable bowel disease is rising at an alarming rate. Some of the diseases of the bowel are degenerative; some have genetic and autoimmune components. All irritable bowel disease can be managed by an *optimal regimen*. But we need to take a hard look at these diseases, because they are affecting more and more Americans.

This chapter ends with a discussion of the challenges facing diabetics. What dietary regimens are most helpful for those suffering from Type I diabetes? How can those afflicted with Type II diabetes overcome the disease? How can we prevent adult-onset (Type II) diabetes? Sixty out of every one thousand Americans have the disease. Nearly half of those people do not even know that they are ill. About one million diabetics suffer from insulin-dependent (Type I) diabetes—the more severe form. Seven million people have been diagnosed with non-insulin-dependent (Type II) diabetes, also called adult-onset diabetes. It is estimated that another eight million people are Type II diabetics but have not yet been diagnosed.

An optimal regimen for those suffering with irritable bowel offers excellent guidelines for the general population. Most of the foods that I consume every day would be ideal for someone who has celiac sprue (gluten intolerance). If I were a celiac, I would need to eliminate intact spelt berries and intact wheat berries (both of which contain gluten), as well as the flour that we mill from those grains. However, I have learned to enjoy a wide variety of grains that do not contain gluten—all of which make lovely muffins, non-yeast bread, and flat bread. There is a whole world of people who consume grains that do not contain gluten and find pleasure in uncomplicated dietary regimens of whole foods. When I look at the long, complicated lists of do's and don'ts for those who have celiac sprue, I cringe. The greatest problems which commonly plague celiacs arise when they ingest gluten accidentally. How does that typically happen? It occurs when celiacs eat processed food. Here are some typical problems: Restaurant french fries may be "cross contaminated" (the same oil for the fries might have been used for breaded fish, chicken, or onion rings containing gluten). Hamburger meat may have been breaded. Highly processed soups and sauces could contain gluten. These convenience foods are high in fat, low in fiber, and they are not good choices for those who seek optimal health.

The point that I am making is this: the problem for celiacs is not merely that of unwittingly consuming gluten in processed food. The significant challenges for celiacs are the same challenges facing the general population. First, discovering what constitutes a healthy diet and a healthy lifestyle, according to the research, requires a major effort; and second, finding the will and wisdom to make radical dietary and lifestyle changes demands a sense of mission. All of us can acquire wisdom and learn to be grateful. Pain and adversity are often our best teachers, but only if we have ears to hear and eyes to see. Americans, in general, are addicted to foods and behaviors that promote disease. The degeneration begins long before most people become symptomatic. Those who suffer from gluten intolerance, as well as other diseases of the bowel, experience pain in response to their dietary choices, while those suffering from other degenerative conditions may have no warning. Heart disease and cancer are silent killers. There is a whole world of food that does not cause the body to degenerate. When we eat whole foods, intact grains, and fresh vegetables, we get all of the micronutrients and fiber that we need. Meeting nutritional needs isn't an ordeal.

The issue that many celiacs (like most people in the general population) do not address is the problem with processed food in general. A celiac can safely order food—first, by requesting whole foods, and second, by requesting that the foods be prepared simply. Here's how I order at Chinese restaurants across the country:

- Fresh vegetables (nothing canned), lightly steamed with absolutely no seasoning
- Extra virgin olive oil on the side (if unavailable, I have my own)
- Garden salad without dressing
- Steamed white rice (the refined rice is a modest compromise while traveling)
- The food is steamed. It hasn't touched a pan or grill with other seasonings. Those with gluten intolerance need not worry about this kind of meal.

Dining out in America can certainly be safe, nutritious, and delightful—if we learn how to make appropriate choices in restaurants that serve real food. In communities across the nation, more and more restaurants feature organic food and specialize in whole food cuisine. In our area we have a whole food supermarket with a deli and a cafeteria that serves delicious whole foods. The vegetables and grains are of excellent quality. Businesses such as these are the true "super" markets, and they are popping up all over the country. A considerable number of consumers have come to understand that organic vegetables of good quality do taste delicious. Many people have also come to know experientially that what they eat impacts the way they feel, on an hour by hour basis. Once we learn what it is like to truly feel great, we are unwilling to indulge in foods that slow us down.

People with seemingly mild cases of irritable bowel (occasional bloating, flatulence, rectal itching, indigestion, and heartburn) need to confine themselves to the kind of simple regimen which I discuss later in the chapter. But so do those individuals who walk around feeling tired most of the time. The most restrictive diet for celiacs is the one recommended by the Celiac Sprue Association/United States of America; the only grains that they recommend as safe for celiacs are rice, wild rice, sorghum, corn, and popcorn. These restrictions probably take into account the problems reported by celiacs who have allergies, food intolerances, and sensitivities that are independent of the gluten intolerance. But celiacs are not alone in their limitations. Each year more and more people find that they cannot tolerate a number of foods—and most of the foods to which they react are nutritionally dense whole foods. They often lack the necessary enzymes to digest food properly, and they lack the proper balance of intestinal flora (insufficient friendly bacteria) to produce additional enzymes and nutrients. Difficulties with digestion and assimilation are widespread. Aids for heartburn, indigestion, diarrhea, constipation, and gastric distress abound in every supermarket, drug store, and convenience market.

We know that many of the symptoms associated with irritable bowel disease afflict the general population. Many people suffer gastrointestinal distress, without seeking more than an over-the-counter remedy that offers symptomatic relief. Most Americans do not consider changes in dietary habits and lifestyle when they begin to suffer physical pain and discomfort. When they seek help from their physicians, patients often receive little or no dietary and lifestyle advice based on the research. And yet, the connection between diet and disease is clear. Once digestion and assimilation of foods become a problem, eating nutrient-dense, high-fiber complex carbohydrates (organic grains and vegetables) may result in pain, flatulence, bloating, allergies, or bleeding. However, those foods are not the *cause* of the problem.

We need to focus on the big picture. If we consider the entire world population, irritable bowel disease, food intolerances, and adult-onset diabetes are rare. We need to ask ourselves why Americans are the world leaders in degenerative disease and what we need to do in order to achieve and maintain optimal health. All of us (not just those who suffer from allergies, food intolerances, fatigue, gastrointestinal disorders, and other degenerative diseases) need to completely digest the foods we eat and fully assimilate the nutrients which those foods offer. Nutritionally dense foods heal our bodies and enable us to overcome debilitating diseases, provided we have the enzymes necessary for complete digestion. If our bodies have not produced sufficient digestive enzymes, we need to take them in supplemental form. We also need to consume fermented foods (soy yogurt, sauerkraut, tempeh, etc.) to nurture and restore the friendly microorganisms in the intestines. Without proper balance in the intestinal flora, we cannot achieve optimal health. I have come to realize that many people who are vitally interested in wellness are too ill to fully digest some of the most vital and nutritious whole foods. Healing foods such as beans, intact grains, raw vegetables, and freshly ground flaxseed will not heal our bodies unless we are able to digest and assimilate them. Those people who are in a degenerative state, after years on the standard American diet, should first begin eating simply, and second, begin supplementing the diet with digestive enzymes and microbial supplements (*Lactobacillus acidophilus, Bifidobacterium bifidum,* etc.).

The Celiac Disease Foundation alerts those who are gluten intolerant to the presence of gluten in specific foods. They encourage celiacs to consider the wide variety of foods that do not contain gluten. Wheat is one of the most overused foods in America. Those who are accustomed to American breads, cereals, and desserts often feel deprived without gluten. I encourage celiacs to focus on building health, not merely avoiding gluten. Processed and devitalized grain products (no matter what the grain) do not build strength and vitality. Such products encourage adult-onset diabetes and other degenerative diseases.

The information on irritable bowel disease, inflammatory bowel disease, and diabetes offers valuable instruction for all of us who want to prevent and cure degenerative disease. Those who suffer from diseases of the bowel, and those who suffer from diabetes, must consume the most powerful foods, and they must make certain that their bodies can digest and assimilate those foods. All of us who are seeking optimal health need that same information.

What about the special needs of those who suffer from irritable bowel disease and inflammatory bowel disease? What problems do they face which are common to many of us?

Irritable Bowel Syndrome

Alternative names for this condition are irritable colon syndrome and spastic colon. Many people have recurrent symptoms throughout their lives that include intermittent pain accompanied by constipation or diarrhea (or an alternating occurrence of both). Physicians often suggest that the causes cannot be determined and that there is no "demonstrable disease." The patient's distress, inability to function normally, and physical weaknesses require the physicians to get a thorough history of the patient and follow a careful diagnostic procedure in order to rule out cancer and inflammatory bowel disease, both of which often have similar symptoms. Common diagnostic tests are *sigmoidoscopy* (examination of the colon), *barium X-ray examination,* and *testing of the patient's feces.*

People with irritable bowel suffer from an involuntary muscle movement in the large intestine, in spite of the fact that they have no abnormality in the intestinal structure. Textbook descriptions of the disorder often report that those who suffer from irritable bowel disease neither gain nor lose weight. That is not necessarily true. Mainstream medical sources also state that irritable bowel syndrome does not cause sufferers to become malnourished. That is also incorrect.

Gastroenterologists report that more than half the patients they see suffer from irritable bowel syndrome, and it is the most common disorder of the intestine. It is also the most common of all chronic disorders. Some experts suspect that far more than 20 percent of the population suffers from irritable bowel. Many sufferers consider their discomfort insignificant. However, bloating, flatulence, and incessant rectal itching cause many others great embarrassment. When we back away from the disease-centered focus of medicine, as it is practiced in the United States, and consider the dietary and lifestyle habits of healthy people throughout the world, irritable bowel syndrome is not a baffling problem. The protocols for overcoming distress are, indeed, comprehensible.

How many people suffer from this syndrome? Again, an estimated 15 to 20 percent of the adult population experiences some degree of bowel irritation. Out of the two million Americans affected by the disease, some report as many as 10 percent may be children. This is not surprising in light of the fact that we are the world leaders in degenerative disease. After examining the connection between commonly consumed foods and disease, those who are willing to make the necessary dietary and lifestyle changes have every reason to hope for healing and restoration.

Those suffering from irritable bowel complain most often about bloating and abdominal cramping. Suffering is temporarily relieved by bowel movements or by passing gas. Many people with irritable bowel syndrome never feel as though they have had a complete evacuation of the bowel. They often have mucus in the feces and discomfort, or pain, after each meal. As a result of poor digestion and assimilation, sufferers experience a wide range of symptoms secondary to bowel irritation: dizziness, nervousness, fatigue, loss of memory, anxiety, depression, palpitations, heartburn, back pain. The list goes on.

What do physicians frequently prescribe? Patients who experience constipation are offered bulk-forming agents such as bran. Drugs are prescribed to relieve spasms and to treat prolonged bouts of diarrhea. The long-term effects of wheat bran, antispasmodic drugs, and antidiarrheal drugs are not positive. Although physicians recommend medication and dietary fiber in order to alleviate suffering (in the short-term), such remedies are not useful in curing irritable bowel syndrome.

Diverticulosis

Diverticulosis is a condition in which the inner lining of the intestine, or other organs, protrudes and creates small sacs (diverticula). A wide range of symptoms and complications characterize this disease. The diverticula usually affect the lower part of the colon (the main section of the large intestine).

Twenty percent of the patients with diverticulosis are symptomatic. Patients suffer from the same symptoms as those with irritable bowel syndrome. Many people have both conditions. Physicians need to rule out cancer if patients have symptoms of diverticulosis. Hemorrhage is rare, but possible. Physicians prescribe fiber supplements and antispasmodic drugs for treatment.

Diverticulitis is the result of inflammation and perforation of the diverticula. The diverticula that are inflamed and perforated cause pain and fever. Treatment includes rest and antibiotics. In severe cases, patients are fed intravenous fluids. In cases of peritonitis (inflammation of the lining of the abdomen), or if perforation causes a large abscess, surgery is often necessary. When surgery is required, the diseased section is removed and the remaining sections are joined together. Some patients require a temporary colostomy. A colostomy is a procedure that contrives an artificial anus at the body surface where it meets part of the large intestine. Obviously, the time to get alarmed is when diverticula are discovered and before diverticulosis becomes symptomatic. But one should never give up hope for healing and restoration, no matter how great the degeneration.

Colitis and Ulcerative Colitis

Colitis is simply an inflammation of the colon. Conventional medical texts suggest that viral infections, bacterial infections such as *Campylobacter*, and even amoebas, may produce toxins which irritate the lining of the colon. A course of antibiotic therapy may kill the friendly bacteria, upset the balance of power in the gastrointestinal region, and thereby cause a form of colitis to occur. Of course, antibiotics kill the friendly bacteria as well as the harmful bacteria, but they also create antibiotic-resistant pathogenic bacteria.

> Scientists at the Federal Centers for Disease Control and Prevention in Atlanta, and all over the world, have been sounding alarm bells about the growth of antibiotic resistance, a problem that has been fueled by patients who demand antibiotics for every bout of the sniffles and by doctors who give in to such demands. The list of dangerously virulent drug-resistant microbes is growing all the time . . . Perhaps the greatest obstacle to breaking the cycle of resistance may be economic

rather than scientific. Drug companies, which are in business to make money, might be expected to market these new antibiotics aggressively, trying to persuade doctors to prescribe them as often as possible. But such rampant prescribing practices create the same problem all over again.[3]

Physicians often treat *Campylobacter* infections with erythromycin. Drugs are also used to treat amebic infections and *Clostridium* infections. There is a better way. The protocols outlined in the next section offer safe, effective, and natural ways to restore health in the region of the gut. Friendly bacteria and pathogenic bacteria, hundreds of different species, coexist in the intestine—and they number in the billions. Lactic acid bacteria impart nutritional and therapeutic benefits: "The antimicrobial substances produced by these bacteria control the proliferation of undesired pathogens."[4] By using probiotic formulas with guaranteed potencies, we can build health while resisting the pathogens. Scientific journals are filled with natural solutions to a wide range of tormenting diseases. Drug therapies (except in emergency cases) ought never to be considered without first exploring the full range of safe and effective natural therapies.

Ulcerative colitis is a chronic condition that affects between forty and fifty people per one hundred thousand. The main symptoms are bloody diarrhea and feces containing pus and/or mucus. The inflammation and ulcers in the lining of the colon and rectum occur in the final stages of irritable bowel disease. The standard treatments to control the disease are corticosteroid drugs (which reduce the inflammation), sulfasalazine, and salicylate derivatives of sulfasalazine. If the inflammation is severe and uncontrollable, the conventional medical solution is the surgical removal of the colon (colectomy). Those who suffer from the inflammation of ulcerative colitis for many years are at risk for cancer.

Recently, I spoke to a parent asking about alternative treatments for an eleven-year-old child with ulcerative colitis. The family lived in another state. The father felt certain that his child could be healed, and a colectomy was not the answer.

When I spoke to the mother, who had watched the child suffer on an hour by hour basis for years, I could understand her exasperation with what she called alternative methods. A variety of "natural healing therapists" had advised her and "practiced" on her child. She had given the child a course of herbal medicines. She had agreed to the child having acupuncture. She had made what she considered to be drastic dietary changes. Nothing improved the child's condition except drugs and, eventually, surgery. Neither the parent nor the child had ever received accurate information concerning the ways in which food intolerances cause irritation to the bowel; they had never spoken to anyone who could tell them exactly how to proceed and why. By the time I met the mother on the telephone, she did not believe that dietary changes could change her child's life. Physicians had advised her that those people who are predisposed metabolically to diseases such as irritable bowel syndrome, ulcerative colitis, and Crohn's disease could not be set free from pain and inflammation simply by embarking on a specific dietary regimen. They spoke of the colectomy as a cure for her child's disease. During a time of crisis with her child, drugs and surgery seemed to her the safest and most rational course of treatment. She wanted an immediate end to the pain for both her child and herself. I prayed with the mother and offered my love and compassion. I had not met her soon enough to offer insight and information.

Why do people in western industrialized countries experience diseases of the bowel while people in developing countries do not? The answers are relatively simple to understand. Diseases of the bowel are, for the most part, caused by dietary and lifestyle habits. Preventing and curing these diseases requires that we understand the connection between dietary and lifestyle habits, and disease. It also requires that we find the will to change our lives. We need spiritual and emotional maturity to arise and make changes in our lives. We need to stand back and look at ourselves in context with American culture and in relationship with the rest of the world. We need to humble ourselves in order to learn how to live.

Crohn's Disease

Crohn's disease is often described as a chronic inflammation of the small bowel. The disease can actually affect any part of the gastrointestinal tract from the mouth to the anus. The most common site of the inflammation is at the end of the small intestine. Researchers indicate that some people are genetically predisposed to the disease.

An increasing number of diseases are being discussed in terms of one's genetic predisposition, or inherited tendency, to develop a particular disease. If two people both have the same inherited tendency, or genetic predisposition, what enables one to stay well and the other to acquire the disease? What is it that pushes us over the edge? In underdeveloped countries, where people do not have our degenerative diseases, or do not have nearly the same rate of degenerative disease, are any of the people genetically predisposed? There are three to six new cases of Crohn's per year per one hundred thousand people in the United States and in most other *developed* countries. It is important to note that the incidence of the disease has been rising over the last thirty years in the United States. Why? We know that one of the significant findings of the China Project concerns the differences in the disease rates of genetically similar people. In the vast population of genetically similar people in China, people from region to region have very different disease rates, because their dietary and lifestyle habits differ greatly. This study, the largest epidemiological study ever done, underscores the connection between dietary and lifestyle habits, and disease. Why are certain diseases more prevalent in western industrialized countries? We do not eat or live as those who do not have our diseases.

When young people suffer from Crohn's disease, the small intestine is often the area most afflicted. The symptoms of Crohn's disease in adults and children are the same as the symptoms of other irritations of the bowel—abdominal pain and diarrhea. When Crohn's disease affects the colon (large intestine), causing bloody diarrhea, it is often confused with ulcerative colitis. The most serious aspect of Crohn's disease is the increasing difficulty sufferers have in absorbing nutrients in the small intestines. The elderly experience more rectal bleeding with Crohn's. All age groups are susceptible to difficulties involving the anus, such as chronic abscesses and cracks.

Nearly a third of the people with Crohn's disease develop internal fistulas. These abnormal passages make damaging connections between internal organs and the surface of the body, or between two organs. With Crohn's patients, fistulas between the intestine and the skin are common. Often, internal fistulas develop between loops of the intestine. Abscesses develop in about 20 percent of Crohn's patients. These pockets of infection form around the anus or in the abdominal area. Diverse complications from Crohn's disease occur in many distinct parts of the body: ankylosing spondylitis (an inflammation of the spine); eczema (and other skin disorders); arthritis (in different joints in the body); inflammation in various parts of the eye; and, in rare instances, problems develop in the stomach, esophagus, and the duodenum (upper part of the small intestine).

Sulfasalazine and corticosteroid drugs are conventional treatments for the inflammation. Many Crohn's patients are under long-term medical supervision and experience severe attacks requiring hospital care (blood transfusions, intravenous feeding, intravenous drug therapy). As the patient degenerates, damaged parts of the small intestine need to be removed by surgery. Surgeons remove only the most affected part, anticipating degeneration to continue. Continued degeneration then necessitates further surgery. Often, narrow obstructing segments must be removed from the large intestine. Sometimes surgery is indicated for the treatment of abscesses, obstructions, perforations, and severe bleeding suffered by Crohn's patients. Some patients remain stable after surgery. Others do not.

Although the outlook for Crohn's is quite grim from the standpoint of conventional medicine, people are able to manage and even overcome the disease with natural therapies. An outline of protocols following this discussion of the symptoms of irritable bowel and inflammatory bowel disease offers every hope.

Pruritus Ani

Pruritus is the medical term for itching, and *pruritus ani* is the term for itching of the skin around the rectum. Health professionals who are aware of the connection between pruritus ani and irritable bowel disease recognize that it is often a symptom of a digestive disorder, or of lactic acid leaking from the colon. The lactic acid causes pain, itching, and bleeding. The outline of protocols following this discussion details the causes of lactic acid production and suggests possible cures.

Pruritus ani is often mistaken for hemorrhoids rather than recognized as a common symptom of any of the irritable and inflammatory bowel diseases. Often, pruritus ani is a symptom of Crohn's disease or ulcerative colitis. Most victims of colon cancer have pruritus ani. This does not mean that it causes bowel cancer, but rather that it places one at risk for bowel cancer.

For immediate relief from pruritus ani, the sufferer needs to wash the affected area with soap and water. (Hemorrhoids are not relieved by that treatment.) However, soap and water do not eliminate the cause of the problem. Pruritus ani is a signal, warning of something out of balance. The permanent solution is to resolve the digestive problems that cause the pruritus.

Celiac Sprue (gluten enteropathy)

Celiac disease is among the least common irritable bowel diseases. Celiac disease is most common among genetically susceptible Caucasians. According to the Celiac Disease Foundation, at least one in 250 persons in the United States is affected.

Sufferers cannot tolerate gluten, a protein found in wheat, rye, barley, and oats. Research suggests that this is an immunologically toxic response to the ingestion of gluten. This reaction is limited to the lining of the small intestine. The villi, tiny projections that carpet the lining of the small intestines, become flattened in celiac disease. This impairs the body's ability to absorb nutrients. The cells covering the hair-like projections on the villi form the brush border. Digestive enzymes reside there. Without the appropriate enzymes, those with celiac sprue cannot tolerate many foods. As I will discuss later, the major celiac sprue support organizations disagree concerning the foods that are threatening to those who suffer from this disease. Specialists with credentials disagree. The answer for those who suffer is to pay attention to food intolerances, many of which may not be related to gluten. As health is restored, those particular intolerances may be overcome. But what about the symptoms directly related to celiac sprue? Some people with celiac sprue never develop symptoms. Others experience fatigue, weight loss, breathlessness (due to anemia), diarrhea, and abdominal pain. Some celiac sprue patients form a distinctive rash called dermatitis herpetiformis (DH). More than 85 percent of DH patients are sensitive to gluten.

Babies who cannot tolerate gluten usually become symptomatic within six months after first having gluten in the diet. The feces of the child develop a foul smell. The babies experience abdominal swelling as a result of gas, and, as one would expect, the children become quite weak and irritable. Inability to absorb iron properly leads to iron deficiency anemia, and the failure to absorb folic acid often leads to megaloblastic anemia. The babies may vomit profusely and/or develop severe diarrhea, both of which may lead to dehydration and cause serious illness.

Physicians are able to make a conclusive diagnosis of celiac sprue by obtaining a jejunal biopsy. With this biopsy, an instrument removes a small sample of the tissue from the lining of the small intestine. Three different biopsies may be performed: one while the patient is consuming foods which contain gluten; a second, when the patient is on a gluten-free regimen; and a third, after gluten is introduced once again into the diet. Changes in the intestinal lining during the second and third biopsies indicate that gluten intolerance is the problem. The malabsorption of nutrients can be documented by blood testing, urine testing, and testing of the feces.

Celiac sprue patients often consider avoiding gluten as their most important mission. But those who are gluten intolerant must also focus on what is necessary to achieve optimal health. Avoiding gluten solves only part of the problem. Later, we discuss the non-glutenous grains that according to all research have not been reported as troublesome for even the most sensitive celiac. Many non-glutenous grains do cause problems for some celiac sprue patients who have, perhaps, been more compromised immunologically as a result of their disease. Those who are susceptible to food intolerances may experience diarrhea and pain after eating a non-glutenous grain. Their symptoms may mimic symptoms of gluten intolerance. Because the cells covering the intestinal villi have been damaged as a result of celiac sprue, enzyme activity is compromised. Consequently, many people with celiac sprue may experience a wide range of food intolerances secondary to gluten intolerance. This, I believe, is the basis for the controversy between the two national celiac support organizations. Obviously, both groups have a passion for offering information to individuals suffering from gluten intolerance. Both organizations need to focus on the consumption of whole foods as an essential part of an optimal dietary regimen. A truly optimal dietary regimen is the celiac's best hope for overcoming all symptoms of irritable bowel disease and gluten intolerance.

Eliminating the Distress of Irritable Bowel Disease and Inflammatory Bowel Disease

The surest way to regain health and to facilitate healing in the bowel is to eliminate the foods we now know irritate the bowel in certain predisposed individuals. Knowing just what foods, or substances, are intolerable to those with bowel disease is the first step in overcoming the symptoms of irritable bowel disease. Those with active bowel disease should avoid three sugars in particular: (1) fructose, (2) lactose, and (3) alcohol sugars (sorbitol and mannitol). (Those who have read *Health Begins in Him* know that I do not include fruit—and certainly no products containing granulated fructose—in the Phase One regimen.) Many of us perform optimally by eliminating all fruits except the avocado. I also recommend (in

Health Begins in Him and in *The Cookbook, Health Begins in Him*) that those who are overcoming degenerative disease, and who are seeking optimal health, eliminate dairy products from their diet. (The Physicians Committee for Responsible Medicine and Frank Oski, M.D., director of the Department of Pediatrics at Johns Hopkins University School of Medicine, recommend eliminating dairy products as a means of optimizing one's dietary regimen.)[5] As for alcohol sugars, they are not digested by anyone (which makes them calorie-free). Large amounts of alcohol sugar irritate the bowels of all people.

Eliminating these three sugars is the important first step for those who seek to strengthen their bodies and overcome disease. The second step in completely overcoming the symptoms of irritable bowel syndrome and inflammatory bowel disease is finding sources of micronutrients that do not irritate the bowel. Those with irritable bowel are often unable to tolerate many nutrient-rich organic whole foods. Foods that irritate the bowel are not good choices no matter how rich they are in vitamins, minerals, amino acids, and phytochemicals. Whole food concentrates are often the ideal source of micronutrients. The third step in becoming symptom-free, and in overcoming, or managing, irritable bowel disease, is to supplement every meal with digestive enzymes and lactic acid bacteria. Replenishing digestive enzymes is essential for those who have spent most of their lives consuming cooked and processed foods that are totally devoid of all enzymes. Lactic acid bacteria offer innumerable benefits.

The beneficial properties of *Lactobacillus acidophilus* DDS-1 based on research documented in internationally reputable, peer-reviewed journals are as follows:

- Production of enzymes such as proteases, which help digest proteins, and lipases, to digest fat.
- Production of B vitamins which are biocatalysts in food digestion, particularly folic acid and B12 . . .
- Production and/or augmentation of immune bodies and their functions.[6]

Eliminate the Foods That Irritate the Bowel

Fructose, Lactose, and the Alcohol Sugars

Those who suffer from irritable bowel need to start here. For example, nearly a third of those who are gluten intolerant are lactose intolerant as well. Another third cannot tolerate fructose or food containing fructose. In certain individuals with gluten intolerance, fructose and lactose provoke the same symptoms they suffer when they consume gluten. Therefore, in those individuals, lactose intolerance and fructose intolerance are secondary to gluten intolerance.

Crohn's disease is, perhaps, the most serious of the inflammatory bowel diseases. Most people with Crohn's disease improve when fructose, lactose, and the alcohol sugars are eliminated. Those who have not improved after eliminating fructose, lactose, and the alcohol sugars need to make sure that they are following the entire protocol outlined here. First, eliminate the foods and substances that are known to irritate the bowel. That means consuming organic whole foods (with no processed or devitalized foods whatsoever) and supplementing the diet with whole food concentrates. Consuming digestive enzymes and friendly bacteria (probiotic formulations) is essential in managing Crohn's disease optimally and in overcoming the ravages of the disease. If new whole foods, particularly grains, are introduced one at a time, intolerances can be identified. Offending foods ought to be reintroduced into the diet from time to time as the sufferer gains strength. Those who are struggling with this disease may look forward to overcoming food intolerances, as well as the debilitating effects of Crohn's disease itself.

Fructose-containing whole foods that must be eliminated are all of the sweet fruits (apples, bananas, cherries, grapes, melons, peaches, pears, pineapples, etc.). The fruits that do not irritate the bowel are tomatoes and avocados.

Honey and corn sweeteners, and all products containing them, are especially offensive. By eliminating all processed foods and recreational food-like products (carbonated beverages, candy, etc.), the focus changes from disease maintenance to health and restoration.

In *Health Begins in Him* and in *The Cookbook, Health Begins in Him*, I discuss the importance of consuming only those baked goods that are made from freshly milled flour. I also talk about the vital role of intact grains (grains before they are milled or flaked). The healthiest people in the world do not pull their foods off the shelves of supermarkets, processed, devitalized, and loaded with fat and high fructose corn sweeteners. Those with irritable bowel disease should not mourn the fact that they cannot use convenience foods or order from a restaurant menu indiscriminately. While it is true that most of the people in the United States are able to eat whatever they choose without experiencing violent pain, it is not true that they can do so without becoming ill. The fact that our nation is now a world leader in obesity and degenerative disease underscores the consequences of our poor dietary choices.

Fructose from whole foods (e.g., apples, oranges, and bananas) is the most common cause of pruritus ani (rectal itching). The condition is caused by lactic acid leaking from the colon onto the skin surrounding the anus. The body usually produces lactic acid when there are not sufficient enzymes to digest fructose, lactose, sorbitol, or mannitol. Some people are able to overcome this with digestive enzymes. Others must eliminate the sweet fruits altogether. (Avocados are not a problem.)

Why does fructose irritate the bowels of some people and not others?

Most people are able to convert fructose into glucose for energy. However, some people have an inherited metabolic inability to digest fructose. They lack the enzyme necessary to digest fructose. For those individuals, mild to severe symptoms of irritable bowel are caused simply by eating fructose, either from whole foods (e.g., apples, oranges, and bananas) or from devitalized foods containing corn syrup. Fructose is made synthetically from corn. It is twice as sweet as cane sugar and much cheaper. Corn syrup has replaced cane and beet sugar in most processed foods. That probably accounts for some of the increase in the incidence of irritable bowel syndrome. Fructose intolerance is a major cause of the most common symptoms of irritable bowel disease: cramping, diarrhea, intestinal gas, and rectal itching.

The body must convert fructose, lactose, sucrose, and starch to glucose before the body can absorb them and use them for fuel. Sucrose (e.g., cane sugar and beet sugar) causes far less trouble for those with irritable bowel than fructose causes. Sucrose and lactose are disaccharides. The disaccharide molecule has two simple sugars. In sucrose, one is glucose and the other is fructose. In the first step of digestion, the glucose and the fructose are separated. In the second step, fructose is converted to glucose. Those with irritable bowel do not have a problem with step one, separating the glucose and the fructose. As we would expect, some of those who suffer from irritable bowel *do* have trouble with step two, converting the fructose into glucose. However, something in the two-step conversion process of the sucrose holds the key to why sucrose is better tolerated than other sources of fructose.

Glucose

Glucose is the essential fuel for the body. Brain cells depend on glucose for their activity. Glucose is the body's chief source of energy for each cell. Glucose, which is a monosaccharide (simple sugar), comes from the digestion of other carbohydrates. The cells produce a small amount of glucose when they metabolize fats and proteins. When we consume intact grains (grains before they are milled or flaked), the glucose is released gradually into the body. This is especially useful as we age, because the hormones that keep the concentration of glucose within a range that is considered normal begin to work less than optimally. An optimal dietary regimen stabilizes blood sugar levels and helps restore the endocrine system. The hormones that deal with our blood sugar fluctuations are insulin (released by the pancreas when blood sugar levels rise), glucagon (released by the pancreas when blood sugar levels are low), epinephrine (released by the adrenals during times of stress), and corticosteroids (released by the adrenals in response to infection). Consuming complex carbohydrates in the form of intact grains and vegetables supports the endocrine system. Even those who are gluten intolerant have a variety of intact grains from which to choose. Organic, short-grain brown rice (Lundberg Farms is my favorite) is one of the best foods available. Quality short-grain, organic rice such as this has a full, rich flavor.

Why does lactose irritate the bowels of some people and not others?

Lactose (the sugar in milk) is another problem for those who suffer bowel irritation. Many people lack the enzyme necessary to convert lactose to glucose. When lactose is not converted to glucose, it is neither digested nor absorbed. As bacteria in the colon begin to ferment, intestinal gas, bloating, abdominal pain, and diarrhea occur. The lining of the intestine becomes irritated or inflamed. A premium *Lactobacillus acidophilus*, such as DDS-1 patented by Khem Shahani, Ph.D., a world renowned expert in probiotics, would certainly help digest lactose. However, many groups such as the Physicians Committee for Responsible Medicine do not recommend dairy for anyone and certainly not for those who are lactose intolerant. The recipes contained in the last chapter of this book have no animal products except for cold water fish (Alaskan red salmon). The China Project establishes that those who are in a degenerative state (as are most Americans who have been on the standard American diet) are at risk by consuming even a small amount of protein from animal sources. For many people, dairy is an enjoyable habit they feel good about, a food from childhood, and a recreational food. For those individuals, I would urge then to discipline themselves to consume only certified organic dairy products. The most wholesome dairy product in our region comes from the Seven Stars Farm in Phoenixville, PA. Their yogurt contains live cultures (*L. acidophilus* and *B. bifidus*) and certified organic maple syrup. Some other dairy products in health food stores feature non-organic dry milk solids, stabilizers, corn syrup, fructose sweeteners, and artificial flavoring. But the best possible choice, in my opinion, is homemade organic *soy* yogurt. It is creamy, delicious, and

filled with live cultures and phytoestrogens. The Traditional
Healthy Diet Pyramids (Latin, Asian, or Mediterranean), featuring the dietary patterns of various cultures, do *not* suggest
two to three servings a day of dairy products. These Traditional Healthy Diet Pyramids reflect the research indicating
that the healthy dietary regimens of Latin America, Asia, and
the Mediterranean countries do not include such large quantities of dairy.[7]

The United States Department of Agriculture Food Guide
Pyramid continues to reflect business interests, rather than the
current state of clinical and epidemiological research. While
fermented foods have a historic record of health benefits, research indicates problems with modern dairy products. Most
dairy products are laden with hormones and antibiotics; they
can hardly be considered beneficial. Organic dairy products,
especially those that are fermented and contain live cultures,
are traditional foods offering nutritional value. However, the
Physicians Committee for Responsible Medicine does not encourage milk consumption and takes issue with the recommendations indicated on the USDA Food Guide Pyramid:

> The Pyramid reflects the outdated idea that lactose in-
> tolerance is rare. In 1965, scientists in Baltimore dis-
> covered it to be the norm among African Americans,
> and the same soon emerged for those of Asian, His-
> panic, or Native American ancestry. In fact, the only
> racial group that typically tolerates milk sugar is Cauca-
> sians, 85 percent of whom carry a genetic mutation that
> causes the lactase enzymes to persist throughout life.
> That may be no advantage, however, because when lac-
> tose is digested, it releases galactose, a smaller sugar that
> is under investigation for its role in cataracts, infertility,
> and ovarian cancer.[8]

Those who overcome irritable bowel or inflammatory bowel
disease do not want to degenerate in other areas. If we imitate
the healthiest people in the world, we will consume no more
than 7 to 10 percent of our protein from animal sources. I
recommend eating Alaskan red salmon and sardines packed in

spring water, three to four times a week, as reliable sources of EPA and DHA, the omega-3 derivatives. Again, those who choose to consume dairy from time to time would do well to limit themselves to organic, fermented dairy. Delicious plant-based meals offer Americans real hope in making wise dietary changes. The Healthy Traditional Latin American Diet Pyramid, the Traditional Healthy Mediterranean Diet Pyramid, and the Traditional Healthy Asian Diet Pyramid are based on evidence that the delicious, traditional cuisine from these regions offers outstanding health benefits. These pyramids were developed to illustrate geographically the healthy dietary patterns of various regions around the world. Consumers need to know about these pyramids and the organizations that work together to produce them.

> This initiative is an outgrowth of a multiyear conference series, "Public Health Implications of Traditional Diets," jointly organized by Harvard School of Public Health, a United Nations World Health Center Organization/Food and Agriculture Organization (WHO/ FAO) Collaborating Center, and Oldways Preservation & Exchange Trust. These Pyramids, taken as a collection, offer substantive refinements of the United States Department of Agriculture's Food Guide Pyramid, refinements that reflect the current state of clinical and epidemiological research worldwide and our understanding of what constitutes optimal human nutrition status.[9]

The Physicians Committee for Responsible Medicine has this to say about the scientific basis of the USDA Food Guide Pyramid:

> When the Pyramid was unveiled in 1992, it was already out of date. People who ignored its recommendations for meat and dairy, eating none of these products at all, were healthier than those who followed them. Diets conforming to the Pyramid make artery blockages worse, not better, and do nothing at all to prevent cancer.[10]

Many nutritionally oriented physicians have concluded that cow's milk is not suitable for human consumption. The connection between cow's milk and juvenile-onset diabetes (Type I) is clear to many researchers. Others say the evidence is not clear at all. I discuss this topic further in connection with the prevention and cure of diabetes at the end of this chapter. Many physicians also recognize that when their patients remove dairy from their dietary regimens, they are able to eliminate symptoms of asthma, congestion, arthritis, ulcerative colitis, migraine headaches, and other degenerative conditions. Another irrefutable fact is that numerous diseases can be traced to cow's milk (i.e., agents found in cow's milk are passed to humans). Some of the most infamous infectious diseases in milk are Helicobacter pylori, E. coli, and salmonella. Those are only a few of the many.

Sorbitol and Mannitol (Alcohol Sugars)

No one is able to digest alcohol sugars. Large amounts of these sugars will irritate the bowels of anyone consuming them. Sorbitol and mannitol are used as sweeteners in toothpaste, breath mints, diabetic candy, and chewing gum. Manufacturers market these products as "sugar-free." They are calorie-free because they are non-absorbable sugars, but they are certainly not sugar-free. Other popular products that contain sorbitol or mannitol are digestive aids, antacids, processed breakfast cereal, low calorie syrup, and chewable vitamins. Even minute amounts of these sugars can cause profound distress in sensitive individuals.

Gluten

Individuals who are suffering from irritable bowel disease, even though they follow an optimal regimen of whole foods and avoid fructose, lactose, mannitol, and sorbitol, should consider having tests to determine whether or not they suffer from celiac sprue (gluten intolerance). Many people with colitis, Crohn's disease, and other diseases of the bowel also suffer from gluten intolerance. Minute amounts of gluten are toxic to celiacs. A full discussion of celiac sprue is beyond the scope of this book. However, I would like to comment on the contradictory advice offered by the two national support organizations. Those who have been diagnosed with this disease ought to read widely. I am personally interested in the findings and conclusions of both groups. The group with a far more restrictive list of foods that are dangerous to celiac and herpetiformis patients is the Celiac Sprue Association/United States of America, Inc. (P.O. Box 31700, Omaha, NE 68131 Telephone: 402/558-0600). This association warns readers who are gluten intolerant not to consume the following grains: wheat, barley, rye, oats, spelt, semolina, kamut, triticale, quinoa, millet, buckwheat, amaranth, and teff. They provide an annotated list stating where the grains originated and why they are not recommended. They report that no formal research exists regarding the dangers of these particular grains to patients with celiac sprue or dermatitis herpetiformis. However, this organization takes the position that members ought to be warned against using grains on this list if other people have reported adverse reactions to the grains. For example, their research shows that as many as 30 to 40 percent of celiacs report minimal and moderate reactions to amaranth. Another good example of their concern for particular sensitivities is with their recommendation of corn (and pure corn meal) as a good basic grain product for celiacs. To that endorsement of corn they add: "those celiacs who may have a sucrose intolerance are not likely to do well with any type of corn products."[11]

The Celiac Disease Foundation (13251 Ventura Boulevard, Suite #1, Studio City, CA 91604-1838 Telephone: 818-990-2354; Fax: 818-990-2379) commented on the recommendations of another support group (without naming that support group) and shared their thoughts concerning the reasons for the controversy. In their booklet, *Guidelines for a Gluten-Free Lifestyle,* they offer a chart entitled, "Plant Taxonomy in Relation to Celiac Toxicity" developed by Donald D. Kasarda, Ph.D., USDA. The chart offers this information regarding grains and vegetables that are appropriate for celiacs:

These grains are
toxic to celiacs: wheat, rye, barley, oats

These grains are   rice, corn, millet, sorghum,
safe for celiacs: Job's tears, ragi, teff

These plants have not been
tested, but are believed to   buckwheat, quinoa,
be safe for celiacs: amaranth, rhubarb, spinach

I think the comments made by the Celiac Disease Foundation in their fall 1997 newsletter may help celiacs who are confused about which foods will cause them problems and which foods will not.

> Recently, another national celiac support group in the United States published a one-page summary of the "principles of the gluten-free diet." Along with the grains that we all know to avoid, the following are included on their "avoid" list: quinoa, millet, buckwheat, amaranth, teff, as well as non-grain items, canola oil and guar gum. The Celiac Disease Foundation would like to emphasize, that in the opinion of many grain and celiac researchers, none of these foods are a source of "gluten." CDF relies on the expertise of world-renowned grain chemist, Donald D. Kasarda, Ph.D., who has published extensive information on this subject.
>
> Rice syrup also appears on the above referenced document in a secondary "other items to avoid" list on the same summary page. *SOME rice syrups (but not all) are processed with barley enzymes, which leave a small residue that could be harmful to celiacs. Some rice syrups are made from rice and are OK.*
>
> The above inaccuracies, as to what is toxic for celiacs, and what is not, have fueled much confusion in the celiac community. We have been swamped with questions and comments via phone, fax, letters and the Internet.
>
> All of the above ingredients have been reported to give *some* celiacs problems, and they should be avoided by

those particular individuals. These problems may be a result of:

1. Some celiacs may have reactions to certain ingredients due to other allergies, intolerances or sensitivities which are independent of their CD.

2. Cross-contamination may be a problem as a result of the method of manufacturing/processing or carelessness in the kitchen.

3. An ingredient may produce celiac-like symptoms without causing villi damage. The laxative effect of guar gum and mannitol, which are ingredients in some foods, is an excellent example of this reaction.

Readers of this newsletter who have not read my book *Health Begins in Him, Biblical Steps to Optimal Health and Nutrition* would profit, I believe, from my discussion of food intolerances and the rationale behind the Phase One and Phase Two dietary regimens. I recovered from a rather wide variety of problems including numerous food intolerances, rapid weight gain, and severe hypoglycemic episodes.

At the time of my health crisis, I had been following a whole foods regimen for many years. I found myself suddenly weakened, disabled, and unable to care for my husband and four children. In the next section, I discuss an optimal regimen for those with adult-onset diabetes. The regimen simply features the most powerful foods available for those who are in a weakened and degenerative state. It is an excellent protocol to achieve maximum strength and endurance. The regimen is also optimal for celiacs. They need only to avoid the glutenous grains (and of course, any prepared food that might contain gluten). In order to achieve optimal health, we need to eat simply and learn to enjoy the great abundance of foods that strengthen our bodies. Whole foods, which are foods in their natural state, offer us the best hope for recovery and restoration.

Celiacs, like others with irritable bowel disease, may need to eliminate fructose, sucrose, lactose, mannitol, and sorbitol in order to be pain free. They must certainly eliminate them, in my opinion, in order to achieve optimal health. Healthy individuals may be able to consume sucrose in moderation without causing degeneration. Such modest consumption of sugar is almost unheard of in the United States, even by those who suffer from diabetes, hypoglycemia, systemic candidiasis, and other conditions that are worsened by the consumption of simple sugars.

Find Sources of Micronutrients and Macronutrients That Do Not Irritate the Bowel

Many people who are suffering from irritable bowel simply cannot begin with high-fiber foods. I recommend certified organic whole food concentrates. When the juice is extracted from organic raw foods, the micronutrients are immediately available at the cellular level. All of the enzymes that are necessary to digest the food are available in the food when it is in its raw state. Those who suffer from irritable bowel disease and inflammatory bowel disease must often eliminate raw vegetables from their regimen until healing and restoration occurs in the region of the gut.

Many people are too ill to spend time gathering organic raw foods suitable for juicing or to spend time juicing them. I recommend certified organic whole food concentrates for those who seek restoration or who wish to maintain optimal health. Products which meet the highest standards available in whole food concentrates are certified organic, vacuum dehydrated cereal grasses and vegetables.

Dehydrated juice from young barley plants provides one of the widest spectrums of naturally occurring nutrients available in a single source. Older methods of dehydration use corn-based starches, such as maltodextrin, as carriers. Consumers should look for certified organic concentrates that contain no binders, fillers, artificial colors, or preservatives. The natural chlorophyll in the young barley grass brings healing to the irritated and inflamed bowel. By consuming the whole food concentrates, the juice of the plant without the fiber, our bodies are able to readily absorb nutrients. Whole food concentrates are an important healing therapy for those who suffer from irritable bowel disease.

I also recommend vacuum dehydrated juice from certified organic carrots. Consumers should look for carrots containing premium de-oiled soybean lecithin, characterized by its high phospholipid content. Carrots are high in beta carotene which, according to research, is useful in both the prevention and cure of cancer. Again, this is an organic whole food, not an isolated nutritional source of beta carotene. Many readers will recall the news coverage of the study on the effects of beta carotene and vitamin A supplements on lung cancer and cardiovascular disease.[12] The study is described as a multicenter, randomized, double-blind, placebo-controlled primary prevention trial—the Beta Carotene and Retinol Efficacy Trial. It concludes that after an average of four years of supplementation, the beta carotene had no benefit and may have had an adverse effect on the incidence of lung cancer and on the risk of death from lung cancer. I would not advise anyone to take beta carotene supplements. But whole foods and whole food concentrates, which are rich in beta carotene, are useful in the prevention and cure of cancer, heart attacks, strokes, and cardiovascular disease. Carrots are naturally high in beta carotene, vitamin B complex, and vitamins C, D, E, and K. Carrots also contain essential minerals—calcium, copper, magnesium, phosphorus, potassium, and sulfur. Certified organic whole food concentrates deliver us essential nutrients in a pure, safe, dense, and convenient form.

A vacuum dehydrated blend of organic cruciferous vegetables offers a powerful supply of phytonutrients. A whole food concentrate containing cabbage (red, purple, and green), kale, broccoli, parsley, and cauliflower is high in cancer antidotes such as indoles, glucosinolates, and dithiolthiones, as well as chlorophyll, carotenoids, calcium, and other minerals. Alfalfa grass, an excellent whole food concentrate, is rich in vitamin B complex (including biotin and folate) and vitamins A, C, D, E, K, and U. It is an important source of calcium, phosphorus, magnesium, iron, selenium, and zinc. Alfalfa is a source of B12 and of silicon (a mineral which research indicates is important for the development of good teeth, hair, and nails).

Those with irritable bowel disease must consume foods that do not irritate the bowel. The whole food concentrates answer this concern by healing and nourishing the body at the same time.

Where to Begin

Fresh raw vegetables, intact grains, freshly milled grain, and freshly ground flaxseed are foods that prevent and reverse degenerative disease. But the benefits of fiber and complex carbohydrates are only available to those whose gastrointestinal tract is ready to receive them. Those who suffer from irritable bowel disease may undermine their own health and well-being by consuming foods that cause them pain or result in symptoms of irritable bowel disease. Many people must begin the healing process by consuming simple foods. Certified organic whole food concentrates are nutritionally dense (containing essential vitamins, minerals, and amino acids). Most important, they are non-irritating to the bowel. Organic white rice and organic flaxseed oil supply the macronutrients (protein, carbohydrates, and fats). They are also well tolerated by those in acute stages of irritable bowel disease. Even though the fiber and outer layer of the rice (containing many of the nutrients) have been removed, the grain still contains protein, carbohydrates, and some nutrients. Often we must begin eating very simply in order to overcome degenerative disease. Each person must become aware of the healing process and appreciate improvements in his or her own body. If we are determined to do what we can in order to walk in wellness, we are more likely to recognize the great significance of even small changes.

Supplement Every Meal with Digestive Enzymes and Friendly Bacteria

The Necessity of Digestive Enzymes

Processed, devitalized foods, as well as whole foods that have been cooked, no longer contain the enzymes necessary for digestion. This places an extra burden on our bodies to produce those missing enzymes. Individuals who are weakened, ill, or simply advancing in years, cannot rely on their bodies to meet this challenge. In our country, we have a growing number of people of all ages who do not properly digest and assimilate the foods they eat. Consequently, those people suffer from food allergies, food intolerances, and fatigue. A failure to digest and assimilate food weakens the immune system, leads to degenerative disease, and reduces life expectancy. Optimal digestion of food and assimilation of micronutrients is essential for optimal health.

After spending months talking with experts in this field, including Khem Shahani, Ph.D. (Professor in the Department of Food Science and Technology at the University of Nebraska), I understood what might constitute an ideal digestive complex. Such a formula would contain amylase, invertase, glucoamylase, protease, malt diastase, cellulase, another protease, peptidase, lipase, lactase, and acid-stable protease. Such a digestive complex is life-changing for those with irritable bowel disease. Digestive enzymes are important for anyone who wants to optimize his digestion and assimilation of cooked and processed foods.

Probiotics—The Key to the Second Immune System

The vital role of fermented food and lactic acid bacteria has never been taught to, or experienced by, most Americans. For centuries, people in much of the world have preserved food with lactic acid bacteria. Last year, while on a medical mission trip to the Ukraine, I was delighted to discover the great number of fermented foods that the Eastern Europeans consume throughout the year. I also realized why they are able to remain free of bacterial infections, in spite of the ways in which meat and dairy products are handled in the markets (all of which are outdoors in many towns). As an American accustomed to the *illusion* of safety in the handling of meat, chicken, fish, and dairy products in the United States (e.g., refrigeration, plastic wrap, and neat labels), I cringed at the thought of people eating foods that would make most Americans ill. In fact, those on our team did get ill and required a variety of medications. The Ukrainians we met didn't suffer gastrointestinal distress. Obviously, they have the necessary microorganisms in their intestines to deal with the challenges they face. Nearly every vegetable they grow in the summer is preserved by fermentation for consumption in the fall, winter, and spring. These strong, hardy people flourish under hardship and deprivation. None of the Ukrainians I met had ever considered the great health benefit in preserving food through fermentation— they fermented food in order to survive the winter. Such survival skills have been passed down to them for centuries. Modern industrialized societies, such as ours, are quick to discard the old ways in favor of the convenient. Count the number of processed, devitalized foods in the health food stores and in whole foods markets. Most people demand instant meals and quick snacks, and they usually aren't longing for a platter of raw vegetables. Fermented foods would be on those shelves if consumers understood the value of microorganisms and purposed to acquire a taste for these extraordinarily beneficial foods. People around the world enjoy fermented foods daily or with nearly every meal.

> It has been well documented that certain types of lactobacilli and bifidobacteria are essential or desirable for optimal health. Metchnikoff [Eli Metchnikoff, *The Prolongation of Life*] was perhaps the first researcher, and he concluded in 1908 that the long life span of the Balkans was due to the ingestion of large quantities of lactobacilli and other lactic organisms through fermented foods, which inhibit pathogens and detoxify their systems.[13]

In the last decade of the twentieth century, we need fermented foods and lactobacilli more than ever. Most people have ingested antibiotics, or consumed meat, poultry, or dairy that has been injected with antibiotics. Thus, the beneficial bacteria in the intestines have been destroyed. Drugs, processed foods, stress, environmental toxins, and impure water can also alter the balance between friendly and harmful bacteria. We must re-establish the friendly bacteria in order to protect ourselves from both infectious and degenerative disease.

In the fall of 1997, Professor Khem Shahani presented a paper to the American College for Advancement in Medicine. This paper is entitled "Nutritional, Therapeutic and Immuno-modulatory Role of Probiotics (Particularly about L. acidophilus DDS-1)." This paper contains an excellent definition of probiotics and a concise explanation of the ways in which the friendly bacteria actually create a second immune system in our bodies. Khem Shahani, Ph.D., is considered to be one of the foremost experts in the world on lactobacilli. Dr. Shahani's comments on probiotics and the "second immune system":

> Our intestines harbor hundreds of species of bacteria, both beneficial and harmful. Probiotics are the micro-organisms which may prevent or reduce the effect of an infection caused by a pathogenic organism. Preponderance of these harmful bacteria in the intestinal tract causes various intestinal disturbances in addition to predisposing the host to various other diseases including ulcers, intestinal cancer, etc. Lactic acid producing bacteria have the ability to kill pathogenic bacteria by secreting small quantities of antibiotic-like substances including lactic acid, acetic acid, benzoic acid, hydrogen peroxide, acidolin, lactocidin and acidophilin. Probiotics are thought to confer a "second immune system" to the host by virtue of their role in preventing pathogens, also by producing B vitamins, improving natural gastrointestinal balance and stimulating immune response.[14]

Irritable bowel disease causes sufferers to be predisposed to cancer. By following the dietary protocols already indicated and supplementing with digestive enzymes and probiotics, the degenerative process can be reversed. In the paper Dr. Shahani presented at the fall 1997 ACAM meeting, he discusses the role of *L. acidophilus* in preventive treatment of colon cancer. Control and experimental groups of rats consumed diets with or without *L. acidophilus* respectively. Both groups were injected with a chemical carcinogen. The results of the experiment indicated that the *L. acidophilus* supplemented group had lower colonic tumor incidence, indicating that bacterium play a role in delaying the initiation of colonic tumors. Dr. Shahani's report detailing the experiment appeared in the *Journal of Applied Nutrition* (volume 48, number 3, 1996).[15]

Perhaps the most widespread symptom of irritable bowel disease is diarrhea. Again, with appropriate dietary protocols, supplementation with whole food concentrates, and use of digestive enzymes and probiotics, the degenerative process can be reversed. Any time there is pain, bloating, or diarrhea, a probiotic supplement is usually necessary and always safe.

> Disturbance in the normal intestinal microflora leads to gastrointestinal disorder, often resulting in diarrhea. Food-borne pathogenic bacteria or their toxins produced in food or in the gastrointestinal tract may cause diarrhea. However, some pathogenic bacteria have to colonize the gastrointestinal tract before the onset of diarrhea. Following colonization by pathogenic bacteria, the numbers of undesired bacteria increase and the numbers of beneficial bacteria, such as lactobacilli and streptococci, decrease. Ingestion of *Lactobacillus acidophilus* and *Streptococcus faecium* supplements or other sources of viable lactobacilli favorably alters the gut microecology. Lactic-acid-producing bacteria also produce antimicrobial substances.[16]

> Feeding infants with viable *B. bifidum* and its growth factors prevented the overgrowth of *Candida albicans* in the gut following penicillin therapy (Mayer, 1966, 1969). Oral administration of *B. bifidum* with a controlled diet has been reported to produce therapeutic effects in infants with bacterial enterocolitis.[17]

Finally, researchers have observed that dietary and supplementary ingestion of *Lactobacillus* species, like *L. acidophilus, L. bulgaricus,* and *L. bifidus,* support the body nutritionally and play a therapeutic role as well. These *Lactobacillus* species produce enzymes that aid in the digestion of proteins, carbohydrates, and fats. They produce B vitamins and enhance the bioavailability of calcium.[18]

Based on Dr. Shahani's research, I recommend that consumers request probiotic products that contain the following microorganisms:

DDS-1 *Lactobacillus acidophilus*
1. DDS-1 is the same strain of *L. acidophilus* for which beneficial properties have been documented in over thirty-five scientific papers published by Khem M. Shahani, Ph.D., and his associates from the University of Nebraska, in internationally reputable journals.
2. DDS-1 is the same strain that is subjected to over thirty rigorous quality controlled tests.
3. DDS-1 is manufactured under the auspices of Khem M. Shahani, Ph.D., from the University of Nebraska.

Lactobacillus bulgaricus
L. salivarius
Bifidobacterium bifidum
B. infantis
Streptococcus faecium
S. thermophilus

The protocols for overcoming irritable bowel syndrome are useful for anyone seeking to achieve optimal health. Those in great pain or experiencing profound inflammation will need to endure a very restrictive diet for a time. But, the encouraging news is that dietary changes can enable sufferers to overcome the debilitating symptoms of irritable bowel disease.

The protocols for the prevention and cure of adult-onset diabetes are the same as the protocols for the prevention and cure of degenerative disease.

Diabetics are at greater risk for atherosclerosis (narrowing of the arteries), hypertension (high blood pressure), and other diseases involving the cardiovascular system. Thus, the regimen that best allows the insulin dependent (Type I) diabetic to control the disease, and clearly enables the non-insulin dependent diabetic (Type II) to reverse the disease, is also a regimen that best helps to prevent adult-onset diabetes and other degenerative diseases as well.

Diabetes Mellitus

Insulin-dependent (Type I) diabetes progresses rapidly and usually manifests itself in people under age thirty-five. It commonly develops in children ten to sixteen years of age. Researchers think that insulin-dependent (Type I) diabetes develops as an immune response to a viral infection. This response may be delayed, resulting years after the damage to the pancreas occurs. Diagnoses of insulin-dependent diabetes have been recorded as having risen sharply after viral epidemics. Mumps and German measles are common viruses associated with diabetes. It is important to recognize that the viruses are not the direct cause of diabetes. Rather, it is widely believed that the immune system mistakes the insulin-secreting cells in the pancreas (beta cells) for the proteins contained in the viruses. The immune system then destroys the beta cells that are similar to the virus particles. When the beta cells are destroyed, the body cannot produce insulin. There are also drugs and chemicals that destroy the body's ability to produce insulin. Two prescription drugs can trigger insulin-dependent diabetes: pentamidine (used to treat pneumonia) and L-asparaginase (a cancer treatment)[19]

Although the causes of insulin-dependent diabetes are not known, articles in the *New England Journal of Medicine* (1992) and the *American Journal of Clinical Nutrition* (1990) indicate that the consumption of cow's milk may be a factor for certain individuals. This is controversial, of course. Imagine the impact on the dairy industry if this were widely believed. Nevertheless, over eighty studies have been published in the last decade implicating the consumption of cow's milk as a cause of insulin-dependent diabetes. Studies indicate that the immune systems of a great number of children cannot differentiate between the cow's milk protein particles and the pancreatic islet cells. Thus, in reacting to the cow's milk, the body destroys the insulin-producing cells as well. Studies showing that high levels of antibodies to the cow's milk protein particles have been found in newly diagnosed diabetics ought to give consumers pause. Certainly, one way to be sure that our supply of calcium is adequate is to avoid calcium-depleting animal proteins (the high phosphorus content of animal products drives calcium out of the body). The other way is to consume calcium-rich foods such as kale, green leafy vegetables, beans, and tofu. These foods are not only rich in vitamins, minerals, and amino acids, they are filled with life-saving phytochemicals as well.

When the cells that secrete insulin are destroyed, the body simply stops producing insulin. Without insulin, sugar cannot get to the cells where it is needed. Regular injections of insulin are necessary in order to prevent the diabetic from going into a coma and dying as a consequence.

Adult-onset diabetes is another matter. The body produces insulin, but the body is resistant to the effects of the insulin. Obesity is often a key factor in developing adult-onset diabetes. Scientists are now predicting that by 2007 one out of every ten people will have adult-onset diabetes. Adult-onset diabetes is considered a chronic illness without a cure, but is it? Although those who develop adult-onset diabetes cannot overcome their symptoms without making significant dietary and lifestyle changes, lifestyle and dietary changes do, indeed, enable sufferers to overcome their illness. Many of us have limitations. If we do not follow an optimal regimen, we suffer in ways that other people do not. However, limitations do not indicate illness, but rather, a greater susceptibility to a particular illness. We need to understand that distinction. Health and wellness are on a continuum. We are on the way to optimal health when we do all that we can, given our challenges and limitations.

Many people suffer from glucose intolerance, an abnormal response to large amounts of sugar. Others suffer, to some degree, from even small amounts of simple sugar. For those individuals, even fruit—in spite of the fact that it contains fiber—causes the blood sugar to rise too rapidly. The symptoms range from headache and fatigue to wet palms and dizziness. As the blood sugar rises rapidly, it causes a sharp insulin response, and then precipitates a hypoglycemic reaction. Dietary and lifestyle changes can break the cycle and restore health and well-being.

Dietary and Lifestyle Changes

We need to get lean and strong by following an optimal dietary regimen (consuming the best fats, unrefined carbohydrates, and plant proteins) and an optimal fitness regimen (aerobic exercise, stretching, and strength training). Whenever we exercise, we need to focus on ways to nourish and detoxify our bodies. Achieving optimal weight is only one aspect of walking in wellness. Simply being thin will not prevent cancer, heart disease, and stroke. Improving both dietary habits and lifestyle is the surest way to prevent and reverse degenerative disease.

> Fat is a problem for diabetics. The more fat there is in the diet, the harder time insulin has in getting sugar into the cell. Exactly why this occurs is not clear. But what is clear is that minimizing fat intake and reducing body fat help insulin do its job much better. Modern diabetic treatment programs drastically reduce meats, high-fat dairy products, and oils. At the same time, they increase grains, legumes, and vegetables.[20]

All of the billions of cells in the body need essential fatty acids. Essential fatty acids (EFAs) enable nutrients to enter the cells. They also maintain the cell membranes, which are actually liquid barriers surrounding the cells. These essential fatty acids are hormone-like substances called prostaglandins. They regulate the immune system, the cardiovascular system, the digestive system, and the reproductive system. Prostaglandins play an essential role in controlling the metabolic rate, the neural circuits in the brain, the healing and repair process, and inflammation. These hormone-like chemicals regulate cellular activity on a moment-by-moment basis.

It is ironic that, as the world leaders in obesity, we are obsessed with fat-free foods and low-fat regimens. The essential fatty acids actually enable our bodies to burn calories. Diabetes is only one of the degenerative conditions that may develop as a result of a fatty acid deficiency. Without the essential fatty acids, we increase our risk of heart disease, cancer, and stroke. We need to limit our fat intake to the essential and beneficial fats; then, we will neither need nor crave the inferior or harmful fats.

There are two families of essential fatty acids. One is the omega-3 family; the other is the omega-6 family. Both are made up of precursors and derivatives. We often speak of the precursors as the "parents," which give birth to the derivatives, or "daughters." Here is how they work:

Alpha-linolenic acid is an omega-3 fatty acid precursor. Our bodies cannot produce alpha-linolenic acid. We must consume foods that contain alpha-linolenic acid. Dark green leafy vegetables are a good source of this omega-3 precursor. Flaxseed oil is also a good source if it is fresh. (Rancid flax oil is without benefit and is harmful.) Organic flaxseed is a safe, rich source of omega-3, because the seed protects the oil until it is ground. (Flaxseed can be ground in seconds by using a small, inexpensive coffee grinder.) Moreover, the whole flax-seed contains lignans that are high in phytoestrogens (plant estrogens). These phytoestrogens protect us from the ravages of xenoestrogens, a topic we have already discussed. Research indicates that the lignans from flaxseed, like the isoflavones in soy, "are converted to biologically active hormone-like substances by intestinal microflora" and "may be cancer protective agents."[21]

Many authors that I admire and enjoy, recommend dark green leafy vegetables as the best source for omega-3 fatty acids. They contend that we do not need to consume the cold water fish (salmon, sardines, mackerel, or herring) in order to obtain omega-3. Their point is that dark green leafy vegetables and flaxseed offer safe, vegetarian choices. However, Edward N. Siguel, M.D., Ph.D. (*Essential Fatty Acids in Health and Disease*), offers vital research that indicates we must sometimes consume foods that contain the omega-3 derivatives.

If we are functioning optimally, are not deficient in micro-nutrients, and are not in a weakened and diseased state—we can produce EPA (eicosapentaenoic acid) and DHA (docosahexaenoic acid), the omega-3 derivatives. However, if our health is compromised in some way, our bodies may not be able to produce the omega-3 fatty acid derivatives (EPA and DHA) from the omega-3 fatty acid precursor (alpha-linolenic acid). In this event, we must consume the EPA and DHA from our food. The cold water fish are excellent sources of fatty acid derivatives. The Center for Science in the Public Interest reports that salmon is the fish most free from contaminants. Many fatty acid researchers consider Alaskan red salmon to be the cold water fish most free of pollutants, and thus the safest to eat. Researchers also suggest that we may benefit by consuming the omega-3 derivatives directly from food since they produce physiological changes rapidly. When our bodies produce EPA and DHA from the alpha-linolenic acid that we have consumed, the physiological changes in our bodies happen more slowly. It is an issue worth considering. A dietary regimen featuring vegetables, grains, and legumes—with modest servings of cold water fish three or four times a week—is, perhaps, ideal for the general population, as well as for the diabetic.

Linoleic acid is an omega-6 precursor. One of the richest sources of omega-6 fatty acid is the soybean. Whole organic soybeans are very different from the wide range of highly processed food products made from soybeans. I recommend organic whole soybeans and organic tofu, or bean curd, a highly concentrated soybean product. Again, research indicates that isoflavones in soybeans may be powerful cancer-protective agents. The high intake of soybeans, according to research, may account for the low mortality in breast and prostate cancer of Japanese women and men, respectively.[22]

Gamma-linolenic acid (GLA) is an omega-6 derivative. If our bodies are not able to produce GLA from linoleic acid, then we must consume the GLA directly from food sources or nutritional supplements. Borage oil, black currant seed oil, and evening primrose oil are good sources of GLA, and they are widely available in softgel form.

Consume the Essential Fatty Acids Every Day

What foods do I eat every day in order to get a reliable supply of essential fatty acids? First, I begin and end the day with dark green leafy vegetables in the form of raw salads and as whole food concentrates (the juice of dehydrated barley grass, alfalfa grass, broccoli, kale, etc.). I also consume at least two tablespoons of organic golden flaxseed (freshly ground) each morning. These are all excellent sources of alpha-linolenic acid, the omega-3 fatty acid precursor. Then, to be sure that I am getting sufficient EPA and DHA (the omega-3 derivatives), I eat Alaskan red salmon (fresh if possible) three to four times a week. Each day I eat either organic whole soybeans or organic tofu (soybean curd). Tofu is a staple in our home, and our children enjoy preparing and serving tofu in a variety of ways (see *The Cookbook, Health Begins In Him*). Soybeans are my favorite source of omega-6 because they are multifunctional (i.e., the soy isoflavones serve as cancer-protective agents, and the soybeans themselves offer an excellent supply of omega-6 fatty acids). Rather than wonder whether or not my body is producing adequate supplies of the omega-6 derivative (gamma-linolenic acid), I consume GLA from borage oil in a softgel capsule.

Most Americans are deficient in the omega-3 fatty acids. No one can achieve optimal health without an adequate supply of omega-3 fatty acids. And yet, many of the therapeutic regimens that help reverse adult-onset diabetes (as well as cardiovascular disease, rheumatoid arthritis, memory loss, and hypertension) do not contain sufficient fatty acids. They are dangerously low (10 percent or less) in fat. We don't need to trade in one infirmity for another. A truly optimal diet will enable those who are ill to reverse a wide range of illnesses. Udo Erasmus, Ph.D., an international authority on fats and oils, says this about regimens deficient in omega-3 fatty acids:

> Diets containing less than 5 percent fats are correlated with cancer in places like the Philippines, most likely due to impaired absorption of vitamins A and E, which protect against cancer-causing free radicals.

> W3s [omega-3s] have been shown to inhibit tumor incidence and growth. Pritikin and Ornish's diets are low in w3s [omega-3s], to which they pay no attention at all. The fats in their diet programs contain essential

fatty acids, (EFAs), but there may not be enough of them because of low total fat content.[23]

Most people have an imbalance in fatty acid metabolism, because they consume too many omega-6 oils and trans-fatty acids. Other people simply do not consume sufficient omega-3 fatty acids because they are purposefully restricting fat in the diet. Udo Erasmus suggests a diet containing 15 to 20 percent of calories as fat, with one-third to one-half of the fat being essential fatty acids. Udo Erasmus points out that although Pritikin overcame obesity and clogged arteries with his now famous dietary regimen, Pritikin battled leukemia and then died in his sixties as a result of suicide. His autopsy revealed that his arteries were clean, but did his diet have sufficient cancer-protective benefits? Flaxseed, a premium source of omega-3 and fiber, has lignans that serve as cancer-protective agents. Soybeans are a premium source of omega-6 and have isoflavones that serve as cancer-protective agents. The key here is to consume those fats that are vital, and to consume them in sufficient quantities. We need a clear understanding of which fats are useful, which fats are harmful, and why.

Another important type of fat: monounsaturated fatty acid rich, extra virgin olive oil

It is important not to squander our allotment of fat grams on meat, poultry, dairy, and fish (other than the cold water fish), because we need to spend those fat grams on the fats that truly build health. In connection with a diet rich in unrefined, high-fiber plant foods, low in saturated fats, and high in essential fatty acids—the diabetic, like everyone else seeking to overcome degenerative disease, can profit from extra virgin olive oil. The Mediterranean diet pyramid offers us a cultural model for healthy eating based on the dietary habits of those who lived in Crete, throughout much of the rest of Greece, and across southern Italy in the 1960s. In this region, "adult life expectancy . . . was among the highest in the world, and the rates of coronary heart disease, certain cancers, and some other diet-related chronic diseases were among the lowest in the world in the early 1960s, despite limitations of existing medical services."[24] Unlike northern European diets that featured animal fats, this Mediterranean region's principle source of fat was olive oil. Meanwhile, Americans in the 1960s believed that meat and milk were two of the most important foods for optimal health and nutrition. Textbooks followed the lead of the United States Department of Agriculture Guidelines and taught American children the importance of meat and dairy in an optimal dietary regimen. When the USDA introduced the Four Food Groups in 1956, they put into effect a dietary model based on business interests. This plan drastically increased the recommended amount of fat and cholesterol in meals. The plan did not reflect any known epidemiological studies, but rather validated the marketing efforts of the meat and dairy industries. Today, we have the 1992 USDA Food Guide Pyramid that offers too few changes, too late.[25]

Research suggests many reasons why extra virgin (unrefined) olive oil is beneficial:

1. Unlike saturated fat, oleic acid is considered anti-thrombotic.
2. Diets high in monounsaturated fats are less likely to be involved in the oxidation of low-density lipoproteins (LDLs)—a process that is thought to increase coronary heart disease—than are diets high in polyunsaturated fat.
3. Certain short-term clinical studies have indicated that substituting olive oil for carbohydrates increases the concentrations of high-density lipoproteins (HDLs) without increasing LDLs. Researchers expect that would reduce coronary risk.
4. Mediterranean people have used extra virgin (crude) olive oil as their major dietary fat for several thousand years, and there is no evidence of harm. The use of polyunsaturated oils is recent and widespread, and the long-term effects are unknown.
5. "Olive oil facilitates the typical consumption of large amounts of vegetables and legumes throughout much of the Mediterranean region by enhancing taste and energy density."[26]

The proportion of energy from total fat in Mediterranean diets varied throughout the region from 28 percent in southern Italy to as much as 40 percent in Crete and other parts of Greece. Two striking points are:

1. The proportions of energy from fat represent diets in which most of the fat was derived from olive oil.[27]
2. This hearty consumption of olive oil characterized the dietary regimen of a population with an adult life expectancy that was among the highest in the world and with rates of coronary disease, certain cancers, and some other diet-related chronic diseases that were among the lowest in the world.[28]

What kind of olive oil did they consume in that region in the 1960s? It was extra virgin quality, made from a simple, traditional process. It was made without heat and still contained all of the natural qualities unique to olives. Extra virgin olive oil has not been degummed, refined, bleached, and deodorized. If the olive oil is not labeled "extra virgin," then it is refined.

> When these protected unsaturated fatty acids are heated above 150° C (302° F), not only do they lose their protective effects, but they also become mutation-causing themselves. Virgin olive oils are the *only* mass-market oils that have not been heated above 150° C.[29]

Udo Erasmus also makes the case that the "minor" (about 2 percent) components of virgin (unrefined) olive oil have major health benefits.

- Beta carotene (pro-vitamin A) and vitamin E (88 percent in the form of alpha-tocopherol)
  Both protect the heart and arteries.
- Magnesium-rich chlorophyll
  This mineral protects the heart.
- Squalene, the main hydrocarbon present in olive oil, and a precursor to phytosterols
  Boosting phytosterols offers increased protection for the heart.

- Phytosterols

  "Phytosterols protect against cholesterol absorption from foods."

- Polyphenols

  Polyphenols are potent antioxidants that protect the heart. Oleoeuropein lowers blood pressure.[30]

The more fat in the diet, the harder time the body has in getting insulin to the cells. In light of the vital role of the essential fatty acids (both the omega-3 and omega-6 precursors and derivatives) and the numerous benefits of extra virgin olive oil, it is necessary to avoid polyunsaturated oils whose long-term effects are unknown.[31] Diabetics, as well as those who suffer from any degenerative disease, can ill afford to consume animal fat (apart from cold water fish). What are the other healthy fats that diabetics need in order to achieve optimal health? The foods that dominate the dietary regimens of the healthiest people in the world—beans, grains, vegetables, and fruit (the avocado)—contain the fats that we need. All of these foods are high in fiber, dense in nutrients, and rich in phytochemicals.

The epidemiological studies clearly show us that Asian, Latin, and Mediterranean cuisine have these benefits in common: the foods are minimally processed, fresh, and seasonal; their dishes contain small amounts of, or no, animal protein; and beans, grains, and vegetables are served one or more times daily.

Notes

1. Chen J., Campbell, T.C., Li J., Peto R., *Diet, Life-style, and Mortality in China, A Study of the Characteristics of 65 Chinese Counties.* Oxford University Press, (Oxford, U.K.), Cornell University Press (Ithaca, NY), Peoples Medical Publishing House (Beijing PRC), 920 pp., 1990.

2. W.C. Willett, F. Sacks, A. Trichopoulou, G. Drescher, A. Ferro-Luzzi, E. Helsing, D. Trichopoulos, "Mediterranean Diet Pyramid: A Cultural Model for Healthy Eating," *American Journal of Clinical Nutrition* 61, no. 6 suppl (1995): 1402S.

3. Sheryl Gay Stolberg, "Superbugs," *New York Times,* 2 August 1998, Section 6, pp. 44, 47.

4. C.F. Fernandes, K.M. Shahani, and M.A. Amer, "Therapeutic role of dietary lactobacilli and lactobacillic fermented dairy products," *FEMS Microbiology Reviews* 46 (1987): 343.

5. Physicians Committee for Responsible Medicine, *Cancer Prevention and Survival Series: Food Choices for Health* (Washington, DC, 1993); Frank A. Oski, M.D., *Don't Drink Your Milk* (Brushton, NY: TEACH Services, 1996).

6. Khem M. Shahani, Ph.D., "Facts and Fallacies about Probiotics" (Lincoln, NE), A position paper distributed privately by Khem M. Shahani, Ph.D., Professor of Food Science and Technology, University of Nebraska.

7. Oldways Preservation and Exchange Trust, "The Healthy Traditional Latin American Diet Pyramid" (Graphic), 1996, "The Traditional Healthy Asian Diet Pyramid" (Graphic), 1995, "The Traditional Healthy Mediterranean Diet Pyramid" (Graphic), 1994 (Cambridge, MA).

8. Neal Barnard, M.D., "The Pyramid Scheme: Racial Bias in Food Guidelines," *Good Medicine,* (Newsletter, Physicians Committee for Responsible Medicine), autumn 1997, 2.

9. Oldways Preservation & Exchange Trust, *The Traditional Healthy Mediterranean Diet Pyramid,* Booklet (Cambridge, MA: Oldways Preservation & Exchange Trust, 1997), 1.

10. Barnard, "The Pyramid Scheme: Racial Bias in Food Guidelines," 2.

11. Celiac Sprue Association/United States of America, Inc., "Update on Grains and Flours" (Omaha, NE).

12. Gilbert S. Omenn, et al., "Effects of a Combination of Beta Carotene and Vitamin A on Lung Cancer and Cardiovascular Disease," *New England Journal of Medicine* 334, no. 18 (1996): 1150-1155.

13. Shahani, "Facts and Fallacies about Probiotics."

14. Khem M. Shahani, Ph.D., "Nutritional, Therapeutic and Immunomodulatory Role of Probiotics (Particularly about L. aci-

dophilus DDS-1)," paper presented at the fall convention of the American College for Advancement in Medicine, Anaheim, CA, 1997, p. 9.

15. Ho Lee, Ph.D., Nagendra Rangavajhyala, Ph.D., Carter Grandjean, Ph.D., and Khem Shahani, Ph.D., "Anticarcinogenic Effect of *Lactobacillus Acidophilus* on N-Nitrosobis(2-oxopropyl)amine Induced Colon Tumor in Rats."

16. Custy F. Fernandes, et al., "Control of Diarrhea by Lactobacilli," *Journal of Applied Nutrition* 40, no. 1 (1988), 32.

17. Custy F. Fernandes, and Khem M. Shahani, "Modulation of Antibiosis by Lactobacilli and Yogurt and Its Healthful and Beneficial Significance," In Proceedings of the National Yogurt Association (New York, NY), May 1989, p. 155.

18. Khem Shahani, H. Fernandes, and V. Amer, "Immunologic and Therapeutic Modulation of Gastrointestinal Microecology by Lactobacilli," *Microecology and Therapy*, 18 (1989): 103-104.

19. "Diabetes: Health and Research Guide," *Ability Magazine* 98, no. 4 (1998).

20. Physicians Committee for Responsible Medicine, "Diet and Diabetes" (Washington, DC).

21. Herman Adlercreutz, Yaghoob Mousavi, Jim Clark, et al., "Dietary Phytoestrogens and Cancer: *In Vitro* and *In Vivo* Studies," *Journal of Steroid Biochemistry and Molecular Biology* 41, no. 3-8 (1992): 331-337; Herman Adlercreutz, Hideo Honjo, Akane Higashi, et al., "Urinary Excretion of Lignans and Isoflavonoid Phytoestrogens in Japanese Men and Women Consuming a Traditional Japanese Diet," *American Journal of Clinical Nutrition* 54 (1991): 1093-1100.

22. Adlercreutz, Honjo, Higashi, et al., "Urinary Excretion," 1093.

23. Udo Erasmus, *Fat That Heal, Fats That Kill* (Burnaby, BC, Canada: Alive Books, 1993), 210.

24. Walter C. Willett, et al., "Mediterranean Diet Pyramid: A Cultural Model for Healthy Eating," *American Journal of Clinical Nutrition*, 61, no. 6, suppl (1995): 1402S.

25. Barnard, "The Pyramid Scheme: Racial Bias in Food Guide-lines."

26. Willett, et al., "Mediterranean Diet Pyramid: A Cultural Model for Healthy Eating," 1404S.

27. Ibid., 1404S.

28. Ibid., 1402S.

29. Erasmus, *Fats That Heal, Fats That Kill,* 254.

30. Ibid., 255-256.

31. Willett, et al., "Mediterranean Diet Pyramid: A Cultural Model for Healthy Eating," 1404S.

International Whole Foods Cuisine
Twenty-One Delicious Recipes for LIFE!

Whole foods chef and baker,
Brian Larson
(under the direction of Terry Dorian),
created seven breakfasts, seven lunches, and
seven dinners that lay a foundation for
an optimal dietary regimen.

Day One

Breakfast

Spelt Waffles

1 ¾ cups freshly milled spelt flour (from 1 cup whole spelt)
2 tablespoons golden flaxseed, finely ground
½ teaspoon sea salt
1 tablespoon non-aluminum baking powder (Rumford)
¼ cup firm tofu
2 tablespoons brown rice syrup
1 ¼ cups water or soy milk
¼ cup soy milk powder (omit if liquid soy milk is used)
2 tablespoons unsweetened applesauce
olive oil cooking spray
pure maple syrup (optional)

• Mix spelt flour, flaxseed, salt, and baking powder in bowl.
• Blend tofu and rice syrup with a fork or a whip; add to flour mixture.
• Add water, soy milk powder, and applesauce; mix well. Let mixture set for 2 to 3 minutes until it becomes light and foamy.
• Spray waffle maker with olive oil cooking spray and cook immediately. Re-spray before each waffle.
• Serve, topping with pure maple syrup if desired.

Alternate method: If using wheat instead of spelt, add an additional 1½ tablespoons of water.

Lunch

Balance and Power Salad

To save time, cut the cabbage into wedges and then slice in a food processor fitted with the shredder attachment.

3 cups thinly sliced, tightly-packed Napa cabbage
1 cup coarsely grated carrot
4 dates, cut into thin strips
4 thinly sliced scallions (green onions)
¼ cup organic raisins
½ cup cooked intact spelt grains (optional)
1 cup cooked chickpeas (optional)
1 portion Tahini Dressing (recipe below)
golden flaxseed, 1 tablespoon per serving, freshly ground

- Combine cabbage, carrot, dates, scallions, raisins, spelt, and chickpeas in a large bowl and toss gently.
- Pour Tahini Dressing over salad and gently toss to coat. Chill, covered, for about 30 minutes before serving.
- Transfer salad to serving bowl and serve at once.
- Sprinkle 1 tablespoon ground flaxseed on each individual portion.

Tahini Dressing

Tahini dressing can be made up in double quantity and stored, covered, in the refrigerator for up to 5 days. It can be used as a tasty substitute for butter.

2 tablespoons sesame tahini
2 tablespoons soy yogurt
1 tablespoon honey
1 tablespoon freshly squeezed lemon juice
1 tablespoon stone-ground mustard
1 teaspoon wheat-free tamari (soy sauce)
1 garlic clove, minced

- Combine tahini, soy yogurt, honey, lemon juice, mustard, tamari, and garlic in glass jar with a plastic screw-top lid. Shake well to combine.
- Use immediately or store as directed. Stir or shake well before using.

Dinner

Spelt Pizza with Garden Vegetables

Crust:
2¼ cups freshly milled spelt flour [or wheat]
2 tablespoons golden flaxseed, finely ground
2½ teaspoons non-aluminum baking powder (Rumford)
sea salt to taste, up to ½ teaspoon
pinch of white pepper
2 tablespoons extra virgin olive oil
¾ cup plus 1 tablespoon cold water [2 tbsp. more with wheat]

Toppings:
1 cup thinly sliced leeks
2 garlic cloves, minced
1 cup grated carrots
1 small zucchini, thinly sliced
2 medium tomatoes, cut into ¼ inch thick slices
1 cup asparagus pieces, 1½ inches long
1 cup grated soy mozzarella cheese
2 tablespoons grated soy Parmesan cheese
4 black olives, halved
1 tablespoon extra virgin olive oil

- Preheat oven to 400°F.
- Mix dry ingredients in bowl. Cut in olive oil until mixture resembles fine bread crumbs. Add cold water and mix with wooden spoon until a ball forms and all the flour is incorporated. Turn dough onto a well-floured surface and knead by folding 7 to 10 times. Be careful not to overwork the dough.
- Roll out to a 10-inch circle on a lightly floured surface. Place on an 11-inch pizza pan. Pierce several places with a fork.
- Bake 10 minutes. Remove from oven to cool and reduce heat to 375°F.
- While crust is baking prepare vegetables. Heat a small amount of water over medium-high heat. Add leek and garlic, reduce heat, and sauté, stirring occasionally until leek is soft, about 5 minutes. Add a small amount of water if needed. Stir in carrots and cook 1 minute more. Set aside to cool.

- Spoon leek and carrot mixture onto crust; spread almost to the edge.
- Arrange zucchini in single layer on center of pizza. Arrange tomato on outside edge of pizza. Place asparagus pieces on top of tomatoes. Sprinkle cheese over vegetables. Sprinkle olives on top of cheese.
- Bake until crust is cooked and topping is golden brown, 20 to 25 minutes.
- Drizzle extra virgin olive oil over top. Serve immediately.

Day Two

Breakfast

Rice Pudding with Blueberries

4 cups soy milk
¾ cup short-grain brown rice
1 stick cinnamon
¼ cup brown rice syrup
½ teaspoon ground cloves
½ teaspoon fresh ginger root, minced
zest of one lemon
1 tablespoon arrowroot
1 cup blueberries
freshly ground golden flaxseed

- Combine the soy milk, rice, and cinnamon stick in a medium-sized saucepan or in the top of a double boiler and cook until very soft, about 45 minutes. Remove cinnamon stick.
- While still hot, stir in the brown rice syrup, cloves, ginger, lemon zest, and arrowroot.
- Cool slightly and fold in most of the blueberries. Let stand for 10 minutes to set, and serve topped with a light coating of freshly ground flax and with a few additional blueberries on top.

Lunch

Greek Salad

4 ounces extra firm tofu, cut into ¾ inch cubes
tamari
1 small head of radicchio
1 cup baby spinach leaves
2 medium tomatoes, cut into wedges
½ cup cucumber, sliced
4 kalamata olives, halved
4 medium figs, quartered
1 tablespoon pine nuts or unsalted pistachio nuts
½ cup thinly sliced green bell pepper
1 small red onion, thinly sliced
2 tablespoons freshly ground golden flaxseed

Oil and Lemon Dressing

2 tablespoons extra virgin olive oil
1 tablespoon freshly squeezed lemon juice
1 tablespoon finely chopped fresh oregano
¼ teaspoon black sesame seed

- Marinate cubed tofu in enough tamari to cover for 30 minutes or overnight. Stir to coat all sides.
- To make dressing, combine oil, lemon juice, oregano, and black sesame seed in a glass jar with a lid. Shake well to combine, then chill.
- Tear radicchio leaves into bite-size pieces. Place in a salad bowl and add spinach, tomatoes, cucumber, olives, figs, pine nuts, bell pepper, onion, and marinated tofu.
- Pour dressing over salad and toss gently. Sprinkle with ground flaxseed. Serve immediately.

Note: This dressing can be prepared up to 3 months in advance and stored in the refrigerator until required.

Dinner

Portabella and Broccoli Stir-Fry

8 ounces firm tofu, cut into ½ inch slices
2 large portabella mushroom caps, sliced ½ inch thick
1 large red onion, cut into 12 wedges
2 cloves garlic, minced
1 tablespoon fresh ginger root, cut into thin strips
1 medium red bell pepper, cut into thin strips
3 cups broccoli florets
1½ cup snow peas
2 teaspoons arrowroot
½ cup miso mixed with ½ cup water
short-grain brown rice

Marinade

¹/₃ cup red wine vinegar
¼ cup tamari
2 tablespoons extra virgin olive oil
2 teaspoons grated fresh ginger

Note: Due to the short cooking time of stir-frying, all vegetables should be cut and measured before you begin.

- Slice mushrooms and tofu into thin ½ inch strips, and marinate for 15 to 30 minutes. Drain, reserving marinade.
- Heat ¼ cup marinade in wok on medium-high heat. Add onion and garlic, stir-fry for 1 minute. Add tofu and mushrooms, turning mushrooms until tender; stir-fry for about 3 to 5 minutes.
- Sprinkle in ginger and stir-fry for 1 minute. Stir in red pepper, broccoli, and snow peas, and stir-fry 2 to 4 minutes more, adding reserved marinade as needed to prevent sticking.
- Blend arrowroot with 1 tablespoon miso stock in a small bowl. Stir remaining stock into wok and bring to a boil.
- Stir in arrowroot and stir constantly until sauce thickens. Reduce heat to low and simmer for 1 minute. Serve immediately over brown rice.

Day Three

Breakfast

Scrambled Tofu with Vegetables

1 small yellow squash, thinly sliced
1 small zucchini, thinly sliced
1 small carrot, grated
1 small red onion, finely chopped
12 ounces soft tofu, crumbled
2 tablespoons tamari or to taste
¼ cup finely chopped parsley
1 clove garlic, minced
½ teaspoon Italian seasoning
1 tablespoon extra virgin olive oil
3 tablespoons freshly ground golden flaxseed
4 slices of Spelt Quick Bread (see recipe below)

- Sauté yellow squash and zucchini in a small amount of water for about 3 minutes. Add carrot and onion, and sauté until soft, about 2 minutes.
- Add crumbled tofu and cook gently until the tofu is heated through, about 3 to 5 minutes.
- Stir in the tamari, parsley, garlic, and Italian seasoning, and remove from the heat. Add extra virgin olive oil and freshly ground flaxseed, and toss.
- Spoon the mixture over four slices of the Spelt Quick Bread toast.

Spelt Quick Bread

3 cups freshly milled spelt flour
1 tablespoon non-aluminum baking powder
½ teaspoon sea salt
2 tablespoons thoroughly ground golden flaxseed
¼ cup brown rice syrup
1½ cup soy milk

- Preheat oven to 325°F.
- Blend the spelt flour, baking powder, sea salt, and ground flaxseed.
- Mix the rice syrup and soy milk well, add to the dry ingredients, and stir until just well moistened.
- Pour batter into oiled loaf pan. Let batter stand for 10 minutes.
- Bake 35 to 40 minutes.

Note: Follow directions exactly. Bread should be moist.

Lunch

Tabbouleh with Chapatis

⅔ cup bulgur (see recipe below)
4 thinly sliced scallions (green onions)
2 cups chopped fresh parsley
¼ cup fresh mint, thinly sliced
½ cup cherry tomatoes, quartered
2 tablespoons freshly ground golden flaxseed
Homemade Chapatis (see recipe in this section)

Dressing

3 tablespoons flax oil
¼ cup freshly squeezed lemon juice
1 teaspoon freshly ground black sesame seed
¼ teaspoon sea salt

- Place bulgur in a small bowl. Add water to cover and leave to soak until tender, about 30 minutes.
- Thoroughly drain bulgur in cheesecloth. Squeeze to extract as much water as possible.
- Place bulgur in medium-sized bowl and add scallions, parsley, mint, tomatoes, and ground flaxseed. Mix gently.
- To make dressing, combine flax oil, lemon juice, sesame seed, and salt in a small bowl and whisk to combine.
- Pour dressing over salad and toss gently until evenly coated. Cover and chill in refrigerator for 30 minutes.
- To serve, spoon into a chapati, roll up, and enjoy.

Option: Add a spoonful of chopped pomegranate for a delicious variation.

Bulgur

4 cups water
2 cups intact wheat

- Place water and wheat in medium saucepan. Bring to a boil, then simmer 45 minutes or until tender. Drain. (Water can be used for soup stock).
- Spread wheat on a cookie sheet. Place in a 250°F. oven for 1 hour or until dry.
- Coarsely grind in food grinder or good blender.
- Store in an airtight container.

Dinner

Tofu, Mushroom, and Bean Stir-Fry

1 pound firm tofu
2 tablespoons tamari
2 tablespoons water
1 medium red onion, cut into 12 wedges
6 scallions (green onions), cut into 1-inch pieces
2 stalks celery, thinly sliced diagonally
2 cloves garlic, minced
2 teaspoons thinly sliced fresh ginger
1 cup green beans, snapped in half
4 dried shiitake mushrooms, soaked in warm water for 15 minutes, drained and sliced into ¼ inch thick pieces.
1 pound bok choy, thick stalks removed, thinly sliced
2 tablespoons freshly ground golden flaxseed.
short-grain brown rice, cooked

Marinade

2 tablespoons tamari
3 tablespoons lime juice, freshly squeezed
1 tablespoon flax oil

- Combine marinade in small bowl and blend well.
- Cut tofu into ½ inch cubes, and place in shallow glass dish. Pour in marinade and turn tofu to coat all sides.
- Cover tightly, and marinate in refrigerator for 30 minutes or overnight.
- Heat 2 tablespoons tamari and 2 tablespoons water in large wok or heavy bottomed frying pan. Add onion, and stir-fry until softened. Add scallions, and stir-fry 1 minute more. Add celery, garlic, and ginger, and stir-fry 1 minute more. Add beans, mushrooms, and bok choy, and stir-fry another 2 minutes. Add water as needed to keep from scorching.
- Gently stir in tofu and marinade, reduce heat, cover, and simmer until tofu is heated through (2 minutes). Stir in freshly ground flaxseed.
- Serve immediately over brown rice.

Day Four

Breakfast

Refried Beans with Spelt Chapatis

2 cups dried red or pinto beans
2 cloves garlic, minced
1 medium red onion, finely chopped
½ teaspoon chili powder
¼ cup freshly ground golden flaxseed
2 tablespoons extra virgin olive oil
3 large vine-ripened tomatoes, coarsely chopped
2 tablespoons chopped fresh cilantro
¼ cup water
soy cheese: Monterey Jack and cheddar, grated
Homemade Chapatis (see recipe below)

- Place the beans in a large saucepan with cold water just to cover. Bring to a boil, uncovered, over high heat. Boil for 2 to 3 minutes, remove from the heat, cover, and set aside for at least one hour.
- Drain and rinse the beans; then return them to the saucepan and cover with cold water. Cover and bring to a boil over high heat. Reduce the heat to low and cook the beans until tender, 1 to 1½ hours. Drain well.
- Place the cooked beans in a large bowl and mash well with a fork or potato masher to a coarse consistency. Add fresh garlic and set aside.
- In a small amount of water, sauté the onion with the chili powder until tender. Add beans, reduce the heat to low, and cook, stirring constantly until heated through.
- Set bean mixture aside, add ground flaxseed and extra virgin olive oil, cover, and keep warm.
- Bring the tomatoes, cilantro, and water to a boil. Then, reduce the heat to low and cook uncovered until thick, 10 to 15 minutes.
- To serve: spoon bean mixture into a casserole dish and top with the cheese and tomato mixture. Spoon hot onto Chapatis.

Homemade Chapatis

2 cups freshly milled spelt flour
½ teaspoon sea salt
2 tablespoons olive oil
¾ cup lukewarm water
olive oil cooking spray

* Mix salt into flour.
* Cut olive oil into flour until it resembles fine breadcrumbs.
* Make well in center of mix, add ½ cup water, and mix with wooden spoon. Stir in enough warm water to form stiff dough.
* Place on cool, lightly-floured surface, and form into a ball. Knead until smooth and elastic but not sticky, approximately 5 minutes.
* Place in bowl. Cover with damp cloth and set aside until dough has soft texture, at least 30 minutes.
* Divide dough into 12 equal parts. Knead each piece lightly into small ball. Roll ball on floured surface. Lift and turn regularly to keep round shape about 5 inches in diameter. Keep finished circles covered with damp cloth.
* Spray fry pan with oil as needed. Heat over medium heat until hot enough for drop of water to sizzle.
* Shake pan until bubbles appear on top of chapatis, approximately 1 minute.
* Turn and cook other side. Continue to shake until cooked, approximately one minute.
* Slide onto warm plate, cover, and keep warm.

Lunch

Hummus with Vegetable Platter

¾ cup dried chickpeas, soaked overnight in cold water
juice of 3 large lemons
½ cup tahini
2 cloves fresh garlic, minced
¼ teaspoon sea salt
2 teaspoons flax oil
¹/₈ teaspoon paprika

- Drain and rinse chickpeas. Place in large saucepan with enough cold water to just cover. Cover pan and bring to a boil over high heat. Reduce heat and simmer until tender, about an hour. Drain, reserving liquid and a few whole chickpeas.
- In a blender, process half of chickpeas to a crumbly texture. Scrape down as needed. Add rest of chickpeas and blend into a fine texture.
- Add lemon juice, tahini, garlic, and salt. Purée until smooth. Add reserved cooking liquid 1 tablespoon at a time until mixture resembles a soft dip.
- Place dip in small serving bowl. Cover top with flax oil. Sprinkle with paprika, and garnish with reserved whole chickpeas.
- Serve warm or cold with raw vegetables or Homemade Chapatis (see recipe in this section).

Raw Vegetable Platter

cauliflower florets
baby carrots
snow peas
celery
thinly sliced sweet potatoes
long slices of cucumber
bell pepper strips
radishes
jicama (**hee**-ka-ma), sliced ½" x ½" x 4" long, sprinkled with freshly squeezed lime juice

Dinner

Judith Kendall's Salmon Recipes

Supreme Salmon

2 large sweet potatoes
1 head of broccoli [or 25 green beans]
1 medium Napa cabbage
3 medium leeks, thinly sliced
2 red peppers, cut into strips
1 to 1½ pounds fresh Alaskan salmon
1 tablespoon black sesame seed
1 teaspoon sea salt
freshly ground golden flaxseed
extra virgin olive oil
fresh parsley

- Cut sweet potatoes in half lengthwise, and crinkle cut each half into ¼-inch slices.
- Cut broccoli into spears.
- Slice Napa cabbage into ¼-inch slices.
- Mix sea salt with sesame seed.
- Mix leeks and Napa cabbage. Place half into 9x13 glass baking dish.
- Next, layer half of leeks, and arrange sweet potatoes in a circle over leeks.
- Arrange red pepper strips alternately with broccoli spears in a pinwheel shape over sweet potatoes. Place salmon on top of vegetables and coat with black sesame seed and sea salt.
- Bake at 350°F. until salmon flakes easily, 20 to 25 minutes for 1½-inch thick salmon. After removing from oven, drizzle olive oil over all and add a sprinkling of flaxseed. Tuck fresh parsley around edge of dish and serve.

Dill Salmon

2 pounds fresh Alaskan salmon
3 leeks or 1 red onion, sliced into rings
½ cup fresh dill
1 cup soy sour cream
½ cup soy yogurt
1 tablespoon Dijon mustard
sprigs of dill weed for garnish

- Poach salmon in water with leeks or onion, and ¼ cup fresh dill for 17 to 20 minutes until it flakes.
- To make sauce, combine soy sour cream, soy yogurt, ¼ cup fresh dill, and Dijon mustard; and mix thoroughly.
- Serve over salmon. Top with sprigs of dill weed as garnish.

Day Five

Breakfast

Soy Yogurt

1 quart soy milk
²/₃ cup soy milk powder [or more, if a thicker yogurt is desired]
2 tablespoons arrowroot powder
1 package yogurt starter, or yogurt from the previous batch, at
room temperature

- Place the starter in a small mixing bowl. Preheat yogurt maker.
- Use a whisk to mix approximately one cup of the soy milk with the soy milk powder and arrowroot in a large mixing bowl. Whisk until smooth. Gradually whisk in the remaining soy milk, mixing thoroughly.
- Pour this mixture into a saucepan, and heat over medium heat to 190°F. (just below boiling), stirring often to prevent it from burning and sticking to the bottom of the pan.
- Remove the pan from the heat, and let it sit undisturbed for a while until the film floating on the top has started to solidify. Carefully remove and discard the film, then stir to cool. You also can set the pan in cold water to cool it faster. Cool to 110°F.
- Pour a little of the milk mixture into the bowl with the starter, and gently, but thoroughly, mix it. Pour this mixture into the saucepan with the milk, and gently, but thoroughly, mix it. Pour this into the yogurt maker container. Cover and let it sit entirely undisturbed for 8 to 10 hours.
- Once finished, place the covered container in the refrigerator and leave it undisturbed for at least 4 to 6 hours.
- After it is cooled and before you add any flavoring, save 3 tablespoons of yogurt as starter for your next batch.

Lunch

Adzuki Bean Salad

This is a delicious salad with a fresh garden taste. For a Tex-Mex flavor, replace the parsley and celery with fresh cilantro and chopped red onion, throw in a jalapeño (chopped) if you dare, and wrap in a chapati with some rice.

½ cup adzuki beans
1 carrot, sliced or cubed
1 tomato, chopped
1 stalk celery, sliced
1 green or red pepper, chopped
¼ cup minced fresh parsley
1 cup (2 ounces) soy provolone or mozzarella cheese, cubed
Homemade Chapatis (see recipe in this section) or short-grain
    brown rice

Dressing:

¼ cup flax oil
¼ cup olive oil
3 tablespoons red wine vinegar
2 cloves garlic, minced
salt and pepper to taste

- Place adzuki beans in medium-sized saucepan, and add water to cover 2 inches above top of beans. Bring to a boil over high heat; then, simmer for 45 minutes to an hour until tender.
- Drain and rinse cooked beans.
- Place adzuki beans, carrot, tomato, celery, pepper, parsley, and cheese in medium-sized salad bowl. Toss gently.
- To make dressing, combine oils, vinegar, garlic, salt, and pepper in a glass jar with a plastic screw-top lid, and shake well to combine.
- Pour dressing over bean salad and toss lightly until well combined. Salad can be made the day ahead for better flavor. Store in the refrigerator.
- Serve wrapped in a chapati or over rice.

Dinner

Vegetable Lasagne

Sauce:

15 ounces tomato sauce
1 medium onion, chopped
1 clove garlic, minced
4 ounces mushrooms, sliced
¼ teaspoon dried basil or 1 teaspoon fresh
¼ teaspoon dried oregano or 1 teaspoon fresh

Filling:

1 pound soft tofu, mashed
½ teaspoon dried basil or ½ tablespoon fresh (optional)
2 tablespoons fresh parsley, chopped
1 clove garlic, minced
6 medium zucchini, about 9 inches long
2 large tomatoes, sliced
1 cup soy mozzarella cheese, shredded
2 tablespoons freshly ground golden flaxseed

- Preheat oven to 350°F.
- Combine tomato sauce, onion, garlic, mushrooms, basil, and oregano in small mixing bowl.
- In another bowl, mash tofu, then add basil, parsley, and garlic. Set aside.
- Peel zucchini and cut off ends. Slice zucchini lengthwise into strips.
- Cover the bottom of a 9 x 13" glass baking dish with half of the zucchini strips.
- Spread tofu mixture over zucchini.
- Layer with sliced tomatoes.
- Spread half of tomato sauce mixture over tomatoes.
- Cover with remaining zucchini slices.
- Top with remaining sauce, and sprinkle with soy mozzarella and ground flax.
- Bake, uncovered, 30 to 45 minutes or until zucchini is tender and mixture is hot in center. Let stand 5 minutes before serving.

Option: To replace the zucchini with lasagne noodles, use the recipe, "Spelt Pasta Dough," from *The Cookbook, Health Begins in Him* (by Terry Dorian, Ph.D., with recipes by Rita M. Thomas), page 93.

Note: The filling is also great for stuffed shells.

Day Six

Breakfast

Gourmet Porridge

¾ cup freshly flaked spelt
¾ cup water
¾ cup soy milk
¼ teaspoon ground nutmeg
¼ teaspoon fresh ginger root, minced
2 dried apricots, chopped
2 rings dried pineapple, chopped
1 tablespoon sliced almonds

1½ tablespoons pure maple syrup (optional)
soy milk (optional)

• Combine spelt and water in a saucepan. Bring to boil over medium heat.
• Stir in ¾ cup soy milk and spices, reduce heat to low, and simmer until spelt is tender, about 2 to 5 minutes. Stir frequently.
• Pour porridge into two bowls.
• Divide dried fruits and almonds into two parts, and sprinkle over porridge.
• Add maple syrup and soy milk.

Lunch

Stuffed Winter Squash

4 large acorn squash, about 9 ounces each
1½ cups water
pinch of salt
½ cup short-grain brown rice
1 medium red onion, finely chopped
2 garlic cloves, minced
1½ cups finely chopped mushrooms
1 large tomato, finely chopped
¼ cup sun-dried tomatoes, chopped
¼ cup organic raisins
¼ cup fresh parsley, finely chopped
¼ cup finely chopped pecans
1 teaspoon black sesame seed
2 tablespoons golden flaxseed, freshly ground

- Preheat oven to 350°F. Slice about ½ inch from the top of each squash, and scoop out the seeds.
- Bake squash upside down on baking tray with small amount of water until flesh is almost tender, about 30 minutes.
- In large saucepan, bring water to a boil. Add salt and rice, and simmer, covered, until the rice is tender, 45 to 55 minutes.
- Sauté the red onion and garlic in a small amount of water over medium-high heat until the onion is soft, about 5 minutes.
- Reduce heat, add mushrooms, and cook until tender, about 3 minutes. Add water as needed to sauté. Stir frequently. Add tomato and sun-dried tomatoes, and cook until fresh tomatoes have softened, about 2 minutes longer.
- Place onion, mushroom, and tomato mixture into a large bowl. Stir in the raisins, parsley, pecans, black sesame seed, and the cooked rice.
- Divide rice mixture evenly, and spoon into squash shells.
- Bake until heated through, about 20 minutes.
- Serve topped with freshly ground flaxseed.

Dinner

Black-Eyed Peas and Vegetable Bredie

1 cup black-eyed peas
2 tablespoons tamari
2 tablespoons water
1 medium leek or 1 small red onion, chopped
1 garlic clove, minced
1 teaspoon finely chopped fresh ginger
1 teaspoon ground cardamom
½ teaspoon fennel seeds, ground
¼ teaspoon ground nutmeg
8 ounce sweet potatoes, peeled and cut into 1-inch pieces
2 large tomatoes, chopped
1 medium yellow pepper, cut into 1-inch squares
1 medium green pepper, cut into 1-inch squares
1¼ cups miso
¼ cup no-salt tomato paste
2 cups shredded Swiss chard, tightly packed
½ cup chopped dried apricots
¼ cup chopped fennel, optional
freshly ground golden flaxseed
brown rice
strips of dried apricots
fresh parsley

- In a large pan, cover black-eyed peas with water. Bring to a boil, boil 2 minutes, remove from heat, and let sit for 1 hour.
- Drain and add fresh water to cover. Bring to boil, reduce heat to medium-low, and simmer, covered, until tender, about 40 minutes. Drain and set aside.
- Meanwhile, heat tamari and water in saucepan over medium-high heat. Add leek, garlic, and ginger, and sauté until softened, stirring occasionally (about 5 minutes). Add cardamom, fennel seeds, and nutmeg. Cook about 2 minutes to develop flavor. Add the sweet potatoes, tomatoes, bell pepper, miso, and tomato paste. Bring to a boil, stirring frequently. Reduce heat, cover, and simmer until vegetables are tender, 20 to 25 minutes.

- Stir in black-eyed peas, Swiss chard, chopped apricots, and fennel
- cover, and cook until tender, about 5 minutes. Serve over rice. Sprinkle with freshly ground flaxseed, and garnish with strips of dried apricots tossed with parsley tips.

Day Seven

Breakfast

Baked Muesli

2 cups freshly flaked oats
1 cup freshly flaked barley
1 cup freshly flaked rye
2 cups freshly flaked spelt
½ cup diced dried apples or pears
½ cup organic raisins
½ cup slivered almonds
⅓ cup pumpkin seeds

Toppings (amounts given are per serving)

¼ to ½ cup Soy Yogurt (see recipe, p. 183)
1 tablespoon freshly ground golden flaxseed
fruit or juice (choose one of the following)
  1 banana, sliced
  ½ cup fresh pineapple, diced
  1 fresh peach, sliced
  ½ apple or pear, grated
  ½ cup blueberries or raspberries
  ⅓ cup freshly made juice (any combination of apple, grape, grapefruit, orange, and pear)

- Preheat oven to 275°F. Place the flaked oats, barley, rye, and spelt on an ungreased cookie sheet. Bake grain mixture for 15 to 20 minutes until a very lightly toasted color appears. Pull from oven and allow to cool.
- Mix in the dried apples or pears, raisins, almonds, and pumpkin seeds.
- Transfer the mixture to a large glass jar with an airtight lid.
- Pour ½ cup of the muesli into a cereal bowl. Add the yogurt, freshly ground flaxseed, and fruit or juice topping of your choice.

Lunch

Stuffed Baked Sweet Potatoes

Choose large, close-to-oval sweet potatoes for stuffing.

4 large sweet potatoes, 6 to 8 ounces each
2 green onions, sliced
½ cup grated soy cheddar cheese, plus extra for garnish
1 tablespoon fresh ginger root, minced (1-inch piece)
1 teaspoon ground cumin
1 teaspoon ground coriander
1 clove fresh garlic, minced
2 tablespoons freshly ground golden flaxseed
salt to taste

soy yogurt (see recipe in this section)
fresh chives or fresh cilantro for garnish

- Preheat oven to 400° F
- Wash sweet potatoes. Prick their skins in several places with a fork.
- Arrange sweet potatoes on oven shelf so not touching, and bake until tender, about 45 minutes.
- Remove from oven, and set aside until cool enough to handle.
- Slice about ½ inch off the top of each sweet potato. Scoop out flesh and mash with a fork.
- Place sweet potato shells on a baking sheet.
- Combine sweet potato, green onions, ½ cup grated soy cheddar cheese, ginger, cumin, coriander, garlic, ground flax, and salt in medium-sized bowl. Mix well.
- Spoon equal portions of mixture into sweet potato shells.
- Return filled sweet potatoes to oven. Bake until hot and filling is golden brown on top, about 10 minutes.
- Serve with a dollop of yogurt, and sprinkle with chives or cilantro and grated soy cheddar.
- Serve with a green salad.

Dinner

Minestrone Soup

1 cup dried navy beans or great northern beans
1 cup intact spelt kernels, rinsed [or barley]
8 cups vegetable stock (see following recipe)
1 large red onion, chopped
2 cloves garlic, minced
2 medium carrots, sliced, or 1 cup baby carrots
2 stalks celery, sliced
2 large tomatoes, chopped
¼ small cabbage, thinly sliced
1 medium zucchini, sliced
1 cup green beans, snapped
2 tablespoons fresh parsley, chopped fine
freshly ground golden flaxseed
grated soy Parmesan cheese (optional)

- Place beans in medium saucepan, then add cold water to cover. Bring to a boil, boil 2 minutes. Remove from heat, cover, and set aside for 1 hour.
- Drain and rinse beans.
- In a 5-quart pot, place spelt, vegetable stock, onion, garlic, carrots, celery, and beans. Cover and bring to a boil. Reduce heat to low, and simmer until beans and spelt are tender, about 1½ hours. (If using precooked beans and spelt, reduce cooking time to 30 minutes).
- Add tomatoes, cabbage, zucchini, and green beans. Over medium heat, cover and cook until vegetables are tender, about 15 minutes. Stir in parsley.
- Ladle into bowls and top with freshly ground flaxseed and Parmesan, if desired.

Quick Vegetable Stock[1]

3 quarts purified water
3 medium leeks, sliced
3 large carrots, coarsely chopped
2 stalks celery, chopped
1 medium onion
1 large turnip, coarsely chopped
2 cloves garlic
1 teaspoon basil
5 large sprigs of parsley
1 teaspoon thyme leaves
1 bay leaf
2 teaspoons sea salt

• In an 8-quart Dutch oven, combine all the above ingredients and bring to a boil. Reduce heat and cover. Simmer for 2 hours. Strain and discard vegetables. Makes 2½ quarts of stock. You can freeze extra stock for future soups.

Notes

1. Terry Dorian, Ph.D., with recipes by Rita M. Thomas, *The Cookbook, Health Begins In Him* (Lafayette, LA: Vital Issues Press, 1997), 132.

————————————————— Bibliography

Audio Tapes

Lee, John R., M.D.; with David T. Zava, Ph.D. *The Secrets of Natural Hormone Therapy: Keys to Preventing Women's Most Serious Health Problems.* Harry DeLigter Productions, 1996. Two audio cassettes, 120 minutes.

Bound Volumes

Chen J.; T.C. Campbell; Li J.; and R. Peto. *Diet, Lifestyle, and Mortality in China: A Study of the Characteristics of Sixty-Five Chinese Counties.* Oxford, U.K.: Oxford University Press; Ithaca, NY: Cornell University Press; Beijing, PRC: People's Medical Publishing House, 920 pp., 1990.

Lee, John R., M.D. *Natural Progesterone: The Multiple Roles of a Remarkable Hormone.* Revised ed. Sebastopol, CA: BLL Publishing, 1993, 1997.

Journal Articles

Adlercreutz, Herman; Esa Hamalainen; Sherwood Gorbach; and Barry Goldin. "Dietary Phyto-Oestrogens and the Menopause in Japan." Letter. *Lancet* 339 (1992): 1233.

Adlercreutz, Herman; Hideo Honjo; Akane Higashi; Theodore Fotsis; Esa Hamalainen; Takeshi Hasegawa; and Hiroji Okada. "Urinary Excretion of Lignans and Isoflavonoid Phytoestrogens in Japanese Men and Women Consuming a Traditional Japanese Diet." *American Journal of Clinical Nutrition* 54 (1991): 1093-1100.

Adlercreutz, Herman; Helene Markkanen; and Shaw Watanabe. "Plasma Concentrations of Phyto-Oestrogens in Japanese Men." *Lancet* 342 (1993): 1209-1210.

Adlercreutz, Herman; Yaghoob Mousavi; Jim Clark; Krister Hockerstedt; Esa Hamalainen, Kristiina Wahala; Taru Makela; and Tapio Hase. "Dietary Phytoestrogens and Cancer: *In Vitro* and *In Vivo* Studies." *Journal of Steroid Biochemistry and Molecular Biology* 41, no. 3-8 (1992): 331-337.

Albertazzi, Paola; M.R.C.O.G.; Francesco Pansini, M.D.; Gloria Bonaccorsi, M.D.; Laura Zanotti, M.D.; Elena Forini, Ph.D.; and Domenico de Aloysio, M.D. "The Effect of Dietary Soy Supplementation on Hot Flushes." *Obstetrics and Gynecology* 91, no. 1 (1998): 6-10.

Anderson, James W., M.D.; Bryan M. Johnstone, Ph.D.; and Margaret E. Cook-Newell, M.S., R.D. "Meta-Analysis of the Effects of Soy Protein Intake on Serum Lipids." *New England Journal of Medicine* 333 (1995): 276-282.

Barnes, Stephen, Ph.D.; T. Greg Peterson; and Lori Coward. "Rationale for the Use of Genistein-Containing Soy Matrices in Chemoprevention Trials for Breast and Prostate Cancer." *Journal of Cellular Biochemistry* 22 suppl (1995): 181-187.

Beard, Mary K., M.D. "Atrophic Vaginitis: Can It Be Prevented As Well As Treated?" *Postgraduate Medicine* 91, no. 6 (1992): 257-260.

Bernstein, Leslie; Brian E. Henderson; Rosemarie Hanisch; Jane Sullivan-Halley; and Ronald K. Ross. "Physical Exercise and Reduced Risk of Breast Cancer in Young Women." *Journal of the National Cancer Institute* 86, no. 18 (1994): 1403-1408.

Berrino, Franco; Paola Muti; Andrea Micheli; Gianfranco Bolelli; Vittorio Krogh; Raffaella Sciajno; Paola Pisani; Salvatore Panico; and Giorgio Secreto. "Serum Sex Hormone Levels after Menopause and Subsequent Breast Cancer." *Journal of the National Cancer Institute* 88, no. 5 (1996): 291-296.

Blatt, Meyer H.G., M.D.; Hans Wiesbader, M.D.; and Herbert S. Kupperman, M.D., Ph.D. "Vitamin E and Climacteric Syndrome." *Archives of Internal Medicine* 91 (1953): 792-799.

Bradford, Reagan H., M.D., Ph.D.; Maria Downton, M.S.; Athanassios N. Chremos, M.D.; Alexandra Langendorfer, M.S.; Sandra Stinnett, M.S.; David T. Nash, M.D.; Geraldine Mantell, M.D.; and Charles L. Shear, Dr. P.H. "Efficacy and Tolerability of Lovastatin in 3390 Women with Moderate Hypercholesterolemia" *Annals of Internal Medicine* 118 (1993): 850-855.

Bravo, Gina, Ph.D.; Pierre Gauthier, Ph.D.; Pierre-Michel Roy, M.D.; Helene Payette, Ph.D.; Philippe Gaulin, M.Sc.; Monique Harvey, B.Sc.; Lucie Peloquin, M.Sc.; and Marie-France Dubois, M.Sc. "Impact of a Twelve-Month Exercise Program on the Physical and Psychological Health of Osteopenic Women." *Journal of the American Geriatric Society* 44, no. 7 (1996): 756-762.

Breslau, Neil A.; Linda Brinkley; Kathy D. Hill; and Charles Y.C. Pak. "Relationship of Animal Protein-Rich Diet to Kidney Stone Formation and Calcium Metabolism." *Journal of Clinical Endocrinology and Metabolism* 66, no. 1 (1988): 140-146.

Campbell, T. Colin; Chen Junshi; Thierry Brun; Banoo Parpia; Qu Yinsheng; Chen Chumming; and Catherine Geissler. "China: From Diseases of Poverty to Diseases of Affluence. Policy Implications of the Epidemiological Transition." *Ecology of Food and Nutrition* 27 (1992): 133-144.

Cassidy, Aedin; Sheila Bingham; and Kenneth D.R. Setchell. "Biological Effects of a Diet of Soy Protein Rich in Isoflavones on the Menstrual Cycle of Premenopausal Women." *American Journal of Clinical Nutrition* 60 (1994): 333-340.

Chajes, Veronique; Claude Lhuillery; Wolfgang Sattler; Gert M. Kostner; and Philippe Bougnoux. "Alpha-Tocopherol and Hydroperoxide Content in Breast Adipose Tissue from Patients with Breast Cancer." *International Journal of Cancer* 67, no. 2 (1996): 170-175.

Chang, King-Jen, M.D.; Tigris T.Y. Lee, M.D.; Gustavo Linares-Cruz, M.D.; Sabine Fournier, Ph.D.; Bruno de Lignieres, M.D. "Influences of Percutaneous Administration of Estradiol and Progesterone on Human Breast Epithelial Cell Cycle in Vivo." *Fertility and Sterility* 63, no. 4 (1995): 785-791.

Chirawatkul, Siriporn; and Lenore Manderson. "Perceptions of Menopause in Northeast Thailand: Contested Meaning and Practice." *Social Science Medicine* 39, no. 11 (1994): 1545-1554.

Chren, Mary-Margaret, M.D.; and Seth Landefeld, M.D. "Physicians' Behavior and Their Interactions with Drug Companies: A Controlled Study of Physicians Who Requested Additions to a Hospital Drug Formulary." *Journal of the American Medical Association* 271, no. 9 (1994): 684-689.

Cumming, Robert Graham. "Calcium Intake and Bone Mass: A Quantitative Review of the Evidence." *Calcified Tissue International* 47 (1990): 194-201.

Dalery, Karl, M.D.; Suzanne Lussier-Cacan, Ph.D.; Jacob Selhub, Ph.D.; Jean Davignon, M.D.; Yves Latour, M.D.; and Jacques Genest, Jr., M.D. "Homocysteine and Coronary Artery Disease in French Canadian Subjects: Relation with Vitamins B12, B6, Pyridoxal Phosphate, and Folate." *American Journal of Cardiology* 75, no.16 (1995): 1107-1111.

Dalton, Katharina "Prenatal Progesterone and Educational Attainments." *British Journal of Psychiatry* 129 (1976): 438-442.

Derzko, Christine M., M.D. "Role of Danazol in Relieving the Premenstrual Syndrome." *Journal of Reproductive Medicine* 35, no 1-suppl. (1990): 97-102.

Elakovich, Stella D.; and Joan M. Hampton. "Analysis of Coumestrol, a Phytoestrogen, in Alfalfa Tablets Sold for Human Consumption." *Journal of Agricultural and Food Chemistry* 32 (1984): 173-175.

Feinleib, Manning, M.D., D.P.H. "Breast Cancer and Artificial Menopause: A Cohort Study." *Journal of the National Cancer Institute* 41, no. 2 (1968): 315-329.

Fernandes, Custy F., Ph.D.; and Khem M. Shahani, Ph.D. "Lactose Intolerance and Its Modulation with *Lactobacilli* and Other Microbial Supplements." *Journal of Applied Nutrition* 41, no. 2 (1989): 51-64.

Fernandes, Custy F., Ph.D.; Khem M. Shahani, Ph.D.; and M.A. Amer, Ph.D. "Control of Diarrhea by *Lactobacilli*." *Journal of Applied Nutrition* 40, no. 1 (1988): 32-43.

Fernandes, Custy F., Ph.D.; Khem M. Shahani, Ph.D.; and M.A. Amer, Ph.D. "Therapeutic Role of Dietary *Lactobacilli* and *Lactobacillic* Fermented Dairy Products." *FEMS Microbiology Reviews* 46 (1987): 343-356.

Follingstad, Alvin H., M.D. "Estriol, the Forgotten Estrogen?" *Journal of the American Medical Association* 239, no. 1 (1978): 29-30.

Fong, Alice K.H.; and Mary J. Kretsch. "Changes in Dietary Intake, Urinary Nitrogen, and Urinary Volume across the Menstrual Cycle." *American Journal of Clinical Nutrition* 57 (1993): 43-46.

Freudenheim, Jo L.; James R. Marshall; John E. Vena; Rosemary Laughlin; John R. Brasure; Mya K. Swanson; Takuma Nemoto; and Saxon Graham. "Premenopausal Breast Cancer Risk and Intake of Vegetables, Fruits, and Related Nutrients." *Journal of the National Cancer Institute* 88, no. 6 (1996): 340-348.

Frisch, R.E.; G. Wyshak; N.L. Albright; T.E. Albright; I. Schiff; K.P. Jones; J. Witschi; E. Shiang; E. Koff; and M. Marguglio. "Lower Prevalence of Breast Cancer and Cancers of the Reproductive System among Former College Athletes Compared to Non-Athletes." *British Journal of Cancer* 52 (1985): 885-891.

Gambrell, R. Don, Jr., M.D. "Use of Progestogens in Postmenopausal Women." *International Journal of Fertility* 34, no. 5 (1989): 315-321.

Garland, Cedric; Elizabeth Barrett-Connor; Arthur H. Rossof; Richard B. Shekelle; Michael H. Criqui; and Paul Oglesby. "Dietary Vitamin D and Calcium and Risk of Colorectal Cancer: A Nineteen-Year Prospective Study in Men." *Lancet* (February 1985): 307-309.

Grady, Deborah, M.D., M.P.H.; Tebeb Gebretsadik, M.P.H.; Karla Kerlikowske, M.D.; Virginia Ernster, Ph.D.; and Diana Petitti, M.D., M.P.H. "Hormone Replacement Therapy and Endometrial Cancer Risk: A Meta-Analysis." *Obstetrics and Gynecology* 85, no. 2 (1995): 304-313.

Grady, Deborah, M.D., M.P.H.; Susan M. Rubin, M.P.H.; Diana B. Petitti, M.D., M.P.H.; Cary S. Fox, M.S.; Dennis Black, Ph.D.;

Bruce Ettinger, M.D.; Virginia L. Ernster, Ph.D., and Steven R. Cummings, M.D. "Hormone Therapy to Prevent Disease and Prolong Life in Postmenopausal Women." *Annals of Internal Medicine* 117, no. 12 (1992): 1016-1037.

Grodstein, Francine, Sc.D.; Meir J. Stampfer, M.D.; JoAnn E. Manson, M.D.; Graham A. Colditz, M.B., B.S.; Walter C. Willett, M.D.; Bernard Rosner, Ph.D.; Frank E. Speizer, M.D.; and Charles H. Hennekens, M.D. "Postmenopausal Estrogen and Progestin Use and the Risk of Cardiovascular Disease." *New England Journal of Medicine* 335, no. 7 (1996): 453-461.

Hargrove, Joel T., M.D.; Wayne S. Maxson, M.D.; and Anne Colston Wentz, M.D. "Absorption of Oral Progesterone is Influenced by Vehicle and Particle Size." *American Journal of Obstetrics and Gynecology* 161, no. 4 (1989): 948-951.

Harrison, J.D., M.B.; S. Watson, Ph.D.; and D.L. Morris, M.D., Ph.D. "The Effect of Sex Hormones and Tamoxifen on the Growth of Human Gastric and Colorectal Cancer Cell Lines." *Cancer* 63 (1989): 2148-2151.

Harte, Jane L.; Georg H. Eifert; and Roger Smith. "The Effects of Running and Meditation on Beta-Endorphin, Corticotropin-Releasing Hormone and Cortisol in Plasma, and on Mood." *Biological Psychology* 40, no. 3 (1995): 251-265.

Heimendinger, Jerianne; and Mary Ann S. VanDuyn. "Dietary Behavior Change: The Challenge of Recasting the Role of Fruit and Vegetables in the American Diet." *American Journal of Clinical Nutrition* 61, no 6-suppl. (1995): 1397S-1401S.

Helsing, Elisabet. "Traditional Diets and Disease Patterns of the Mediterranean, circa 1960." *American Journal of Clinical Nutrition* 61, no. 6-suppl. (1995): 1329S-1337S.

Hsia, Lily S.Y., C.N.M., M.S., C.P.N.P.; and Maryann H. Long, CNM, MPH. "Premenstrual Syndrome: Current Concepts in Diagnosis and Management." *Journal of Nurse-Midwifery* 35, no. 6 (1990): 351-357.

Hunter, David J., M.B.; JoAnn E. Manson, M.D.; Graham A. Colditz, M.B.; Meir J. Stampfer, M.D.; Bernard Rosner, Ph.D.; Charles H. Hennekens, M.D.; Frank E. Speizer, M.D.; and Walter

C. Willett, M.D. "A Prospective Study of the Intake of Vitamins C, E, and A and the Risk of Breast Cancer." *New England Journal of Medicine* 329, no. 4 (1993): 234-240.

Jordan, V. Craig, Ph.D., D.Sc.; M.H. Jeng, Ph.D.; W.H. Catherino; and C.J. Parker. "The Estrogenic Activity of Synthetic Progestins Used in Oral Contraceptives." *Cancer* 71, no. 4-suppl (1993): 1501-1505.

Karpf, David B., M.D.; Deborah R. Shapiro, Dr. P.H.; Ego Seeman, M.D.; Kristine E. Ensrud, M.D.; C. Conrad Johnston, Jr., M.D.; Silvano Adami, M.D.; Steven T. Harris, M.D.; Arthur C. Santora II, M.D., Ph.D.; Laurence J. Hirsch, M.D.; Leonard Oppenheimer, Ph.D.; and Desmond Thompson, Ph.D.; for the Alendronate Osteoporosis Treatment Study Groups. "Prevention of Nonvertebral Fractures by Alendronate: A Meta-Analysis." *Journal of the American Medical Association* 277, no. 14 (1997): 1159-1164.

Katan, Martijn B.; Peter L. Zock; and Ronald P. Mensink. "Dietary Oils, Serum Lipoproteins, and Coronary Heart Disease." *American Journal of Clinical Nutrition* 61, no. 6-suppl. (1995): 1368S-1373S.

Keys, Ancel. "Mediterranean Diet and Public Health: Personal Reflections." *American Journal of Clinical Nutrition* 61, no. 6-suppl. (1995): 1321S-1323S.

Koskinen, T.; K. Pyykko; R. Kudo; H. Jokela; and R. Punnonen. "Serum Selenium, Vitamin A, Vitamin E, and Cholesterol Concentrations in Finnish and Japanese Postmenopausal Women." *International Journal for Vitamin and Nutrition Research* 57 (1987); 111-114.

Kuiper, George G.J.M.; Eva Enmark; Markku Pelto-Huikko; Stefan Nilsson; and Jan-Ake Gustafsson. "Cloning of a Novel Estrogen Receptor Expressed in Rat Prostate and Ovary." *Proceedings. National Academy of Sciences, U.S.A.* 93, no. 12 (1996): 5925-5930.

Kushi, Lawrence H.; Rebecca M. Fee; Thomas A. Sellers; Wei Zheng; and Aaron R. Folsom. "Intake of Vitamins A, C, and E and Postmenopausal Breast Cancer: The Iowa Women's Health Study." *American Journal of Epidemiology* 144, no. 2 (1996): 165-174.

Kushi, Lawrence H.; Elizabeth B. Lenart; and Walter C. Willett. "Health Implications of Mediterranean Diets in Light of Contemporary Knowledge. 1. Plant Foods and Dairy Products." *American Journal of Clinical Nutrition* 61, no. 6-suppl. (1995): 1407S-1415S.

Kushi, Lawrence H.; Elizabeth B. Lenart; and Walter C. Willett. "Health Implications of Mediterranean Diets in Light of Contemporary Knowledge. 2. Meat, Wine, Fats, and Oils." *American Journal of Clinical Nutrition* 61, no. 6-suppl. (1995): 1416S-1427S.

LeBars, Pierre L., M.D., Ph.D.; Martin M. Katz, Ph.D.; Nancy Berman, Ph.D.; Turan M. Itil, M.D.; Alfred M. Freedman, M.D.; Alan F. Schatzberg, M.D.; for the North American EGb Study Group. "A Placebo-Controlled, Double-Blind, Randomized Trial of an Extract of Ginkgo Biloba for Dementia." *Journal of the American Medical Association* 278, no. 16 (1997): 1327-1332.

Lee, H.P.; L. Gourley; S.W. Duffy; J. Esteve; J. Lee; and N.E. Day. "Dietary Effects on Breast Cancer Risk in Singapore." *Lancet* 337 (1991): 1197-1200.

Lee, Ho, Ph.D.; Nagendra Rangavajhyala, Ph.D.; Carter Grandjean, Ph.D.; and Khem M. Shahani, Ph.D. "Anticarcinogenic Effect of *Lactobacillus acidophilus* on N-nitrosobis(2-oxopropyl)amine Induced Colon Tumor in Rats." *Journal of Applied Nutrition* 48, no. 3 (1996): 59-66.

Lee, John R., M.D. "Osteoporosis Reversal: The Role of Progesterone." *International Clinical Nutrition Review* 10, no. 3 (1990): 384-391.

Lee, John R. "Osteoporosis Reversal with Transdermal Progesterone." Letter. *Lancet* 336 (1990): 1327.

Lemon, Henry M., M.D. "Pathophysiologic Considerations in the Treatment of Menopausal Patients with Oestrogens; The Role of Oestriol in the Prevention of Mammary Carcinoma." *Acta Endocrinologica* 233, suppl (1980): 17-27.

Lemon, Henry M., M.D.; Herbert H. Wotiz, Ph.D.; Langdon Parsons, M.D.; and Peter J. Mozden, M.D. "Reduced Estriol Excretion in Patients with Breast Cancer Prior to Endocrine Therapy." *Journal of the American Medical Association* 196, no. 13 (1966): 1128-1136.

Liberman, Uri A., M.D., Ph.D.; Stuart R. Weiss, M.D.; Johann Broll, M.D.; Helmut W. Minne, M.D.; Hui Quan, Ph.D.; Norman H. Bell, M.D.; Jose Rodriquez-Portales, M.D.; Robert W. Downs, Jr., M.D. Jan Dequeker, M.D., Ph.D.; Murray Favus, M.D.; Ego Seeman, M.D.; Robert P. Recker, M.D.; Thomas Capizzi, Ph.D.; Arthur C. Santora II, M.D., Ph.D.; Antonio Lombardi, M.D.; Raksha V. Shah, M.A., R.D.; Laurence J. Hirsch, M.D.; and David B. Karpf, M.D.; for the Alendronate Phase III Osteoporosis Treatment Study Group. "Effect of Oral Alendronate on Bone Mineral Density and the Incidence of Fractures in Postmenopausal Osteoporosis." *New England Journal of Medicine* 333, no. 22 (1995): 1437-1443.

Liener, Irvin E. "Possible Adverse Effects of Soybean Anticarcinogens." *Journal of Nutrition* 12 suppl (1995): 744S-750S.

Lock, Margaret; Patricia Kaufert; and Penny Gilbert. "Cultural Construction of the Menopausal Syndrome: The Japanese Case." *Maturitas* 10 (1988): 317-332.

London, Robert S.; G.S. Sundaram; Michael Schultz; P.P. Nair; and Phillip J. Goldstein. "Endocrine Parameters and Alpha-Tocopherol Therapy of Patients with Mammary Dysplasia." *Cancer Research* 41 (1981): 3811-3813.

Lurie, Samuel; and Richard Borenstein. "The Premenstrual Syndrome." *Obstetrical and Gynecological Survey* 45, no. 4 (1990): 220-228.

Lyritis, G.P.; N. Tsakalakos; B. Magiasis; T. Karachalios; A. Yiatzides; and M. Tsekoura. "Analgesic Effect of Salmon Calcitonin in Osteoporotic Vertebral Fractures: A Double-Blind Placebo-Controlled Clinical Study." *Calcified Tissue International* 49 (1991): 369-372.

Manson, JoAnn E., M.D.; Meir J. Stampfer, M.D.; Graham A. Colditz, M.B.; Walter C. Willett, M.D.; Bernard Rosner, Ph.D.; Frank E. Speizer, M.D.; and Charles H. Hennekens, M.D. "A Prospective Study of Aspirin Use and Primary Prevention of Cardiovascular Disease in Women." *Journal of the American Medical Association* 266, no. 4 (1991): 521-527.

Martin, Mary C., M.D.; Jon E. Block, Ph.D.; Sarah D. Sanchez, M.Sc.; Claude D. Arnaud, M.D.; and Yewoubdar Beyene, Ph.D. "Menopause without Symptoms: The Endocrinology of Menopause among Rural Mayan Indians." *American Journal of Obstetrics and Gynecology* 168, no. 6 (1993): 1839-1845.

Messina, Mark; and Stephen Barnes. "The Role of Soy Products in Reducing Risk of Cancer." *Journal of the National Cancer Institute* 83, no. 8 (1991): 541-546.

Murkies, A.L.; C. Lombard; B.J.G. Strauss; G. Wilcox; H.G. Burger; and M.S. Morton. "Dietary Flour Supplementation Decreases Post-Menopausal Hot Flushes: Effect of Soy and Wheat." *Maturitas* 21 (1995): 189-195.

National Institutes of Health. "Consensus Conference: Osteoporosis." *Journal of the American Medical Association* 252, no. 6 (1984): 799-802.

O'Brien, Patrick. "Dietary Shifts and Implications for US Agriculture." *American Journal of Clinical Nutrition* 61, no. 6-suppl. (1995): 1390S-1396S.

Omenn, Gilbert S., M.D., Ph.D.; Gary E. Goodman, M.D., M.S.; Mark D. Thornquist, Ph.D.; John Balmes, M.D.; Mark R. Cullen, M.D.; Andrew Glass, M.D.; James P. Keogh, M.D.; Frank L. Meyskens, Jr., M.D.; Barbara Valanis, Dr.P.H.; James H. Williams, Jr., M.D.; Scott Barnhart, M.D., M.P.H; and Samuel Hammar, M.D. "Effects of a Combination of Beta Carotene and Vitamin A on Lung Cancer and Cardiovascular Disease." *New England Journal of Medicine* 334, no. 18 (1996): 1150-1155.

Outwater, J.L.; A. Nicholson; and N. Barnard. "Dairy Products and Breast Cancer: the IGF-1, Estrogen, and bGH Hypothesis." *Medical Hypotheses* 48 (1997): 453-461.

Pak, Charles Y.C., M.D.; Khashayer Sakhaee, M.D.; Beverley Adams-Huet, M.S.; Veronica Piziak, M.D., Ph.D.; Roy D. Peterson, R.N.; and John R. Poindexter, B.S. "Treatment of Postmenopausal Osteoporosis with Slow-Release Sodium Fluoride: Final Report of a Randomized Controlled Trial." *Annals of Internal Medicine* 123, no.6 (1995): 401-408.

Pennington, Jean A.T., Ph.D., R.D.; Barbara E. Young; Dennis B. Wilson; Roger D. Johnson; and John E. Vanderveen, Ph.D. "Mineral Content of Foods and Total Diets: The Selected Minerals in Foods Survey, 1982 to 1984." *Journal of the American Dietetic Association* 86, no. 7 (1986): 876-891.

Prior, Jerilynn C., M.D. "One Voice on Menopause." *Journal of the American Women's Association* 49, no. 1 (1994): 27-29.

Prior, Jerilynn C., M.D. "Progesterone as a Bone-Trophic Hormone." *Endocrine Reviews* 11, no. 2 (1990): 386-398.

Rabin, Douglas S.; Peter J. Schmidt; Gregory Campbell; Philip W. Gold; Margaret Jensvold; David R. Rubinow; and George P. Chrousos. "Hypothalamic-Pituitary-Adrenal Function in Patients with the Premenstrual Syndrome." *Journal of Clinical Endocrinology and Metabolism* 71, no. 5 (1990): 1158-1162.

Rangavajhyala, Nagendra, Ph.D.; Khem M. Shahani, Ph.D.; G. Sridevi; and S. Srikumaran. "Nonlipopolysaccharide Component(s) of *Lactobacillus acidophilus* Stimulate(s) the Production of Interleukin-1a and Tumor Necrosis Factor-a by Murine Macrophages." *Nutrition and Cancer* 28, no. 2 (1997): 130-134.

Raz, Raul, M.D.; and Walter E. Stamm, M.D. "A Controlled Trial of Intravaginal Estriol in Postmenopausal Women with Recurrent Urinary Tract Infections." *New England Journal of Medicine* 329, no. 11 (1993): 753-756.

Reginster, Jean Y., M.D., Ph.D.; Rita Deroisy, Ph.D.; Marie P. Lecart, M.D.; Nathalie Sarlet, M.D.; Brigette Zegels, Ph.D.; Isabelle Jupsin, Ph.D.; Marc de Longueville, M.D.; and Paul Franchimont, M.D., Ph.D. "A Double-Blind, Placebo-Controlled, Dose-Finding Trial of Intermittent Nasal Salmon Calcitonin for Prevention of Postmenopausal Lumbar Spine Bone Loss." *American Journal of Medicine* 98 (1995): 452-458.

Reinisch, June M.; and Stephanie A. Sanders. "Effects of Prenatal Exposure to Diethylstilbestrol (DES) on Hemispheric Laterality and Spatial Ability in Human Males." *Hormones and Behavior* 26, no. 1 (1992): 62-75.

Renaud, Serge; Michel de Lorgeril; Jacques Delaye; Janine Guidollet; Franck Jacquard; Nicole Mamelle; Jean-Louis Martin;

Isabelle Monjaud; Patricia Salen; and Paul Toubol. "Cretan Mediterranean Diet for Prevention of Coronary Heart Disease." *American Journal of Clinical Nutrition* 61, no. 6-suppl. (1995): 1360S-1367S.

Rico, H.; M. Revilla; E.R. Hernandez; L.F. Villa; M. Alvarez de Buergo. "Total and Regional Bone Mineral Content and Fracture Rate in Postmenopausal Osteoporosis Treated with Salmon Calcitonin: A Prospective Study." *Calcified Tissue International* 56 (1995): 181-185.

Rimm, Eric B., Sc.D.; Walter C. Willett, M.D., Dr.P.H.; Frank B. Hu, M.D., Ph.D.; Laura Sampson, M.S.; Graham A. Colditz, M.B., Dr.P.H.; JoAnn E. Manson, M.D., Dr.P.H.; Charles Hennekens, M.D., Dr.P.H.; and Meir J. Stampfer, M.D., Dr.P.H. "Folate and Vitamin B6 from Diet and Supplements in Relation to Risk of Coronary Heart Disease among Women." *Journal of the American Medical Association* 279, no. 5 (1998): 359-364.

Rose, David P. "Diet, Hormones, and Cancer." *Annual Review of Public Health* 14 (1993): 1-17.

Royston, Ivor, M.D.; John L. Sullivan, M.D.; Phillip O. Periman, M.D. and Elliott Perlin, M.D. "Cell-Mediated Immunity to Epstein-Barr-Virus-Transformed Lymphoblastoid Cells in Acute Infectious Mononucleosis." *New England Journal of Medicine* 293, no. 23 (1975): 1159-1163.

Scandinavian Simvastatin Survival Study Group. "Randomised Trial of Cholesterol Lowering in 4444 Patients with Coronary Heart Disease: The Scandinavian Simvastatin Survival Study (4S)" *Lancet* 344 (1994): 1383-1389.

Segal, Shimon; and Robert F. Casper. "Progesterone Supplementation Increases Luteal Phase Endometrial Thickness and Oestradiol Levels in In-Vitro Fertilization." *Human Reproduction* 7, no. 9 (1992): 1210-1213.

Sempos, Christopher T., Ph.D.; Nancy E. Johnson, Ph.D.; Everett L. Smith, Ph.D.; and Catherine Gilligan. "A Two-Year Dietary Survey of Middle-Aged Women: Repeated Dietary Records as a Measure of Usual Intake." *Journal of The American Dietetic Association* 84, no. 9 (1984): 1008-1013.

Setchell, K.D.R.; S.J. Gosselin; M.B. Welsh; J.O Johnston; W.F. Balistreri; L.W. Kramer; B.L. Dresser; and M.J. Tarr. "Dietary Estrogens—A Probable Cause of Infertility and Liver Disease in Captive Cheetahs." *Gastroenterology* 93 (1987): 225-233.

Shaaban, Mamdouh M. "Contraception with Progestogens and Progesterone during Lactation." *Journal of Steroid Biochemistry and Molecular Biology* 40, no. 4-6 (1991): 705-710.

Shahani, Khem M., Ph.D.; H. Fernandes; and V. Amer. "Immunologic and Therapeutic Modulation of Gastrointestinal Microecology by *Lactobacilli*." *Microecology and Therapy* 18 (1989): 103-104.

Shi, Y. Eric; Yiliang E. Liu; Marc E. Lippman; and Robert B. Dickson. "Progestins and Antiprogestins in Mammary Tumor Growth and Metastasis." *Human Reproduction* 9, suppl 1 (1994): 162-173.

Sojka, J.E., V.M.D.; and C.M. Weaver, Ph.D. "Magnesium Supplementation and Osteoporosis." *Nutrition Reviews* 53, no. 3 (1995): 71-80.

Sowers, MaryFran R., Ph.D.; Robert B. Wallace, M.D.; and Jon H. Lemke, Ph.D. "The Association of Intakes of Vitamin D and Calcium with Blood Pressure among Women." *American Journal of Clinical Nutrition* 42 (1985): 135-142.

Spiegel, David; Joan R. Bloom; Helena C. Kraemer; and Ellen Gottheil. "Effect of Psychosocial Treatment on Survival of Patients with Metastatic Breast Cancer." *Lancet* 2 (1989): 888-891.

Stampfer, Meir J., M.D.; Graham A. Colditz, M.B., B.S.; Walter C. Willett, M.D.; JoAnn E. Manson, M.D.; Bernard Rosner, Ph.D.; Frank E. Speizer, M.D.; and Charles H. Hennekens, M.D. "Postmenopausal Estrogen Therapy and Cardiovascular Disease: Ten-Year Follow-Up From the Nurses' Health Study." *New England Journal of Medicine* 325, no. 11 (1991): 756-762.

Stanford, Janet L., Ph.D.; Noel S. Weiss, M.D., Dr.P.H.; Lynda F. Voigt, Ph.D.; Janet R. Daling, Ph.D.; Laurel A. Habel, M.P.H.; and Mary Anne Rossing, Ph.D. "Combined Estrogen and Progestin Hormone Replacement Therapy in Relation to Risk of Breast

Cancer in Middle-Aged Women." *Journal of the American Medical Association* 274, no. 2 (1995): 137-142.

Tavani, Alessandra; and Carlo La Vecchia. "Fruit and Vegetable Consumption and Cancer Risk in a Mediterranean Population." *American Journal of Clinical Nutrition* 61, no. 6-suppl. (1995): 1374S-1377S.

Tew, Bee-Yen; Xia Xu; Huei-Ju Wang; Patricia A. Murphy; and Suzanne Hendrich. "A Diet High in Wheat Fiber Decreases the Bioavailability of Soybean Isoflavones in a Single Meal Fed to Women." *Journal of Nutrition* 126 (1996): 871-877.

Thune, Inger, M.D.; Tormod Brenn, M.Sc.; Eiliv Lund, M.D., Ph.D.; and Maria Gaard, M.D. "Physical Activity and the Risk of Breast Cancer." *New England Journal of Medicine* 336, no. 18 (1997): 1269-1275.

Trichopoulou, Antonia; Antigone Kouris-Blazos; Tonia Vassilakou; Charalambos Gnardellis; Evangelos Polychronopoulos; Michael Venizelos; Pagona Lagiou; Mark L. Wahlqvist; and Dimitrios Trichopoulos. "Diet and Survival of Elderly Greeks: A Link to the Past." *American Journal of Clinical Nutrition* 61, no. 6-suppl. (1995): 1346S-1350S.

Utian, Wulf H., M.D., Ph.D. "Overview on Menopause." *American Journal of Obstetrics and Gynecology* 156, no. 5 (1987): 1280-1283.

Verhoef, Petra; Frans J. Kok; Dick A.C.M. Kruyssen; Evert G. Schouten; Jacqueline C.M. Witteman; Diederick Grobbee; Per M. Ueland; and Helga Refsum. "Plasma Total Homocysteine, B Vitamins, and Risk of Coronary Atherosclerosis." *Arteriosclerosis, Thrombosis and Vascular Biology* 17, no. 5 (1997): 989-995.

Verhoeven, D.T.H.; N. Assen; R.A. Goldbohm; E. Dorant; P. van't Veer; F. Sturmans; R.J.J. Hermus; and P.A. van den Brandt. "Vitamins C and E, Retinol, Beta-Carotene, and Dietary Fibre in Relation to Breast Cancer Risk: A Prospective Cohort Study." *British Journal of Cancer* 75, no. 1 (1997): 149-155.

Wang, C.; and M.S. Kurzer. "Effects of Isoflavones, Flavonoids, and Lignans on Proliferation of Estrogen-Dependent and -Independent Human Breast Cancer Cells." *Proceedings of the American Association for Cancer Research* 37 (1996): 277.

"Warning about Oesophagitis with Fosamax" *Lancet* 347 (1996): 959.

Whitehead, M.I.; T.C. Hillard; and D. Crook, Ph.D. "The Role and Use of Progestogens." *Obstetrics and Gynecology* 75, no. 4-suppl (1990): 59S-76S.

Wiklund, I.; G. Berg; M. Hammar; J. Karlberg; R. Lindgren; and K. Sandin. "Long-Term Effect of Transdermal Hormonal Therapy on Aspects of Quality of Life in Postmenopausal Women." *Maturitas* 14, no. 3 (1992): 225-236.

Wilcox, Gisela; Mark L. Wahlqvist; Henry G. Burger; and Gabriele Medley. "Oestrogenic Effects of Plant Foods in Postmenopausal Women." *British Medical Journal* 301 (1990): 905-906.

Willett, Walter; Frank Sacks; Antonia Trichopoulou; Greg Drescher; Anna Ferro-Luzzi; Elisabet Helsing; and Dimitrios Trichopoulos. "Mediterranean Diet Pyramid: A Cultural Model for Healthy Eating." *American Journal of Clinical Nutrition* 61, no. 6-suppl. (1995); 1402S-1406S.

Wolff, Mary S.; Paolo G. Toniolo; Eric W. Lee; Marilyn Rivera; and Neil Dubin. "Blood Levels of Organochlorine Residues and Risk of Breast Cancer." *Journal of the National Cancer Institute* 85 (1993): 648-652.

The Writing Group for the PEPI Trial. "Effects of Estrogen or Estrogen/Progestin Regimens on Heart Disease Risk Factors in Postmenopausal Women: The Postmenopausal Estrogen/Progestin Interventions (PEPI) Trial." *Journal of the American Medical Association* 273, no. 3 (1995): 199-208.

Zaridze, David; Yelena Lifanova; Dmitrii Maximovitch; Nicholas E. Day; and Stephen W. Duffy. "Diet, Alcohol Consumption, and Reproductive Factors in a Case-Control Study of Breast Cancer in Moscow." *International Journal of Cancer* 48, no. 4 (1991): 493-501.

Ziel, H.K., M.D.; and W.D. Finkle, Ph.D. "Increased Risk of Endometrial Carcinoma among Users of Conjugated Estrogens." *New England Journal of Medicine* 293, no. 23 (1975): 1167-1170.

Transcripts of Live Presentations

Fernandes, Custy F., Ph.D.; and Khem M. Shahani, Ph.D. "Modulation of Antibiosis by *Lactobacilli* and Yogurt and Its Healthful and Beneficial Significance." In Proceedings of National Yogurt Association. New York, May 1989, pp. 145-159.

Shahani, Khem M., Ph.D. " Nutritional, Therapeutic, and Immunomodulatory Role of Probiotics (Particularly about *L. acidophilus* DDS1)." Paper presented at the Fall Convention of the American College for Advancement in Medicine, Anaheim, CA, 1997.

Books

The American Medical Association Home Medical Encyclopedia. 2 vols. Charles B. Clayman, M.D., medical editor. New York: Random House, 1989.

Austin, Phylis; Agatha M. Thrash, M.D.; and Calvin L. Thrash, M.D. *Fatigue: Causes, Treatment, and Prevention.* Sunfield, MI: Family Health Publications, 1989.

Austin, Phylis; Agatha M. Thrash, M.D.; and Calvin L. Thrash, M.D. *Food Allergies Made Simple.* Sunfield, MI: Family Health Publications, 1985.

Barnard, Neal, M.D. *Eat Right, Live Longer: Using the Natural Power of Foods to Age-Proof Your Body.* New York: Crown Publishers, Harmony Books, 1995.

Barnard, Neal, M.D. *Food for Life: How the New Four Food Groups Can Save Your Life.* New York: Crown Publishers, 1993.

Barnes, Broda O., M.D.; and Lawrence Galton. *Hypothyroidism: The Unsuspected Illness.* New York: Harper and Row, Publishers, 1976.

Bland, Jeffrey, Ph.D. *Vitamin C: The Future Is Now.* New Canaan, CT: Keats Publishing, 1995.

Bonk, Melinda. *Controlling Hormones Naturally: My Journey for Solutions to PMS, Menopause, and Osteoporosis with Wild Yam.* Hallandale, FL: MB Publishers, 1996.

Bonvie, Linda; Bill Bonvie; and Donna Gates. *The Stevia Story: A Tale of Incredible Sweetness and Intrigue.* Atlanta: B.E.D. Publications, 1997.

Carper, Jean. *Food—Your Miracle Medicine: How Food Can Prevent and Cure over One Hundred Symptoms and Problems.* New York: HarperCollins Publishers, HarperPerennial edition, 1994.

Carter, J.P. *Racketeering in Medicine: The Suppression of Alternatives.* Hampton Roads Publishing, 1992.

Contreras, Francisco, M.D. *Health in the Twenty-first Century: Will Doctors Survive?* Chula Vista, CA: Interpacific Press, 1997.

Cousins, Norman. *Anatomy of an Illness as Perceived by the Patient: Reflections on Healing and Regeneration.* New York: Norton, 1979.

Crawford, Amanda McQuade. *The Herbal Menopause Book.* Freedom, CA: The Crossing Press, 1996.

Crayhon, Robert. *The Health Benefits of FOS (Frutooligosaccharides): "Fast Food" for the Friendly Bacteria That Keep Us Healthy.* New Canaan, CT: Keats Publishing, 1995.

Dalton, Katharina, M.D. *Once a Month: The Original Premenstrual Syndrome Handbook.* 5th rev. ed. Alameda, CA: Hunter House, 1994.

DeAngelis, Lissa; and Molly Siple. *Recipes for Change: Gourmet Wholefood Cooking for Health and Vitality at Menopause.* New York: Penguin Books USA, Dutton, 1996.

Dorian, Terry, Ph.D. *Health Begins in Him: Biblical Steps to Optimal Health and Nutrition.* Lafayette, LA: Huntington House Publishers, 1995.

Dorian, Terry, Ph.D.; recipes by Rita M. Thomas. *The Cookbook: Health Begins in Him.* Lafayette, LA: Vital Issues Press, 1997.

Erasmus, Udo. *Fats That Heal, Fats That Kill.* 2nd ed. Burnaby, BC, Canada: Alive Books, 1993.

Fonda, Jane; recipes by Robin Vitetta. *Jane Fonda Cooking for Healthy Living.* Atlanta: Turner Publishing, 1996.

Gaby, Alan R., M.D. *Preventing and Reversing Osteoporosis: Every Woman's Essential Guide.* Rocklin, CA: Prima Publishing, 1994.

Gazella, Karolyn A. *Saw Palmetto: Nature's Answer to Enlarged Prostate!* Green Bay, WI: IMPAKT Communications, 1997.

Gittleman, Ann Louise. *Super Nutrition for Menopause.* New York: Simon and Schuster, Pocket Books, 1993.

Greenwood, Sadja, M.D. *Menopause Naturally: Preparing for the Second Half of Life.* 4th ed. Volcano, CA: Volcano Press, 1996.

Hope, Simon. *Cooking for a Healthy Family.* New York: Stewart, Tabori and Chang, 1995.

Hulse, Virgil, M.D. *Mad Cows and Milk Gate.* Phoenix, OR: Marble Mountain Publishing, 1996.

Hunter, Beatrice Trum. *Grain Power: Nutritional Riches of Whole Grains—From Wheat and Rice to Millet, Spelt, and Quinoa.* New Canaan, CT: Keats Publishing, 1994.

Ito, Dee. *Without Estrogen: Natural Remedies for Menopause and Beyond.* New York: Crown Publishers, Crown Trade Paperbacks, 1994.

Jacobowitz, Ruth S. *One Hundred Fifty Most-Asked Questions about Menopause: What Women Really Want to Know.* New York: William Morrow and Company, Quill, 1993.

Jacobowitz, Ruth S. *One Hundred Fifty Most-Asked Questions about Osteoporosis: What Women Really Want to Know.* New York: William Morrow and Company, Hearst Books, 1993.

Kamen, Betty, Ph.D. *Hormone Replacement Therapy: Yes or No?* Novato, CA: Nutrition Encounter, 1993.

Kamen, Betty, Ph.D. *Startling New Facts about Osteoporosis.* Revised ed. Novato, CA: Nutrition Encounter, 1989, 1996.

Lark, Susan M., M.D. *Making the Estrogen Decision: All the Information You Need to Make It—Including the Full Range of Natural Alternatives.* New Canaan, CT: Keats Publishing, 1996.

Lau, Benjamin, M.D., Ph.D. *Garlic and You: The Modern Medicine.* Vancouver: Apple Publishing Company, 1997.

Lau, Benjamin, M.D., Ph.D. *Garlic for Health.* Marion, TX: Lotus Light Publications, 1988.

Laux, Marcus, N.D.; and Christine Conrad. *Natural Woman, Natural Menopause.* New York: HarperCollins Publishers, 1997.

Lee, John R., M.D.; with Virginia Hopkins. *What Your Doctor May Not Tell You about Menopause: The Breakthrough Book on Natural Progesterone.* New York: Warner Books, 1996.

Lee, William H., R.Ph., Ph.D. *The Friendly Bacteria: How Lactobacilli and Bifidobacteria Can Transform Your Health.* New Canaan, CT: Keats Publishing, 1988.

Love, Susan M., M.D.; with Karen Lindsey. *Dr. Susan Love's Hormone Book: Making Informed Choices about Menopause.* New York: Random House, Times Books, 1998.

Marshall, Anne; and Carolyn Kelly. *The World's Healthiest Food.* Ed. Margaret Olds. New York: Stewart, Tabori and Chang, 1996.

Martin, Raquel; with Judi Gerstung, D.C. *The Estrogen Alternative: Natural Hormone Therapy with Botanical Progesterone.* Rochester, VT: Healing Arts Press, 1997.

Martorano, Joseph, M.D.; and Maureen Morgan; with William Fryer. *Unmasking PMS: The Complete Medical Treatment Plan.* New York: Berkley Books, 1994.

McDougall, John A., M.D.; recipes by Mary McDougall. *The McDougall Program for Maximum Weight Loss.* New York: Penguin Books USA, Plume, 1994.

Medical Economics Company. *Physicians' Desk Reference.* 51st ed. Montvale, NJ: Medical Economics Company, 1997.

Moquette-Magee, Elaine, M.P.H., R.D. *Eat Well for a Healthy Menopause: The Low-Fat, High-Nutrition Guide.* New York: John Wiley and Sons, 1996.

Murray, Frank. *Ginkgo Biloba.* New Canaan, CT: Keats Publishing, 1993.

Murray, Frank. *Remifemin: Herbal Relief for Menopausal Symptoms.* New Canaan, CT: Keats Publishing, 1996.

Murray, Michael T., N.D. *Male Sexual Vitality: How You Can Benefit from Diet, Vitamins, Minerals, Herbs, Exercise and Other*

Natural Methods. Getting Well Naturally Series. Rocklin, CA: Prima Publishing, 1994.

Murray, Michael T., N.D. *Menopause: How You Can Benefit from Diet, Vitamins, Minerals, Herbs, Exercise and Other Natural Methods.* Getting Well Naturally Series. Rocklin, CA: Prima Publishing, 1994.

Murray, Michael T., N.D. *Natural Alternatives to Over-the-Counter and Prescription Drugs.* New York: William Morrow and Company, 1994.

Nachtigall, Lila, M.D.; Robert D. Nachtigall, M.D.; and Joan Rattner Heilman. *What Every Woman Should Know: Staying Healthy after Forty.* New York: Warner Books, 1995.

Northrup, Christiane, M.D. *Women's Bodies, Women's Wisdom: Creating Physical and Emotional Health and Healing.* New York: Bantam Books, 1994; Bantam trade paperback edition, 1995.

Ojeda, Linda, Ph.D. *Menopause without Medicine: Feel Healthy, Look Younger, Live Longer.* 2nd revised ed. Alameda, CA: Hunter House, 1992.

Ornish, Dean, M.D. *Dr. Dean Ornish's Program for Reversing Heart Disease.* New York: Random House, 1990.

Oski, Frank A., M.D. *Don't Drink Your Milk.* Brushton, NY: TEACH Services, 1996.

Passwater, Richard A., Ph.D. *The New Superantioxidant-Plus: The Amazing Story of Pycnogenol®, Free-Radical Antagonist and Vitamin C Potentiator.* New Canaan, CT: Keats Publishing, 1992.

Passwater, Richard A., Ph.D. *Selenium Update: How It Protects Against Cancer, Heart Disease, Arthritis and Aging.* New Canaan, CT: Keats Publishing, 1987.

Passwater, Richard A., Ph.D.; and Chithan Kandaswami, Ph.D. *Pycnogenol: The Super "Protector" Nutrient.* New Canaan, CT: Keats Publishing, 1994.

Perry, Susan; and Katherine O'Hanlan, M.D. *Natural Menopause: The Complete Guide to a Woman's Most Misunderstood Passage.* Reading, MA: Addison-Wesley Publishing Company, 1992.

Rako, Susan, M.D. *The Hormone of Desire: The Truth about Sexuality, Menopause, and Testosterone.* New York: Crown Publishers, Harmony Books, 1996.

Richard, David. *Stevia Rebaudiana: Nature's Sweet Secret.* Bloomingdale, IL: Blue Heron Press, 1996.

Robbins, John; recipes by Jia Patton and friends. *May All Be Fed: Diet for a New World.* New York: Avon Books, 1992.

Roehl, Evelyn. *Whole Food Facts.* Rochester, VT: Healing Arts Press, 1996.

Rosenthal, M. Sara. *The Thyroid Sourcebook: Everything You Need to Know.* 2nd ed. Los Angeles: Lowell House, 1996.

Ryneveld, Edna Copeland. *Secrets of a Natural Menopause: A Positive Drug-Free Approach.* St. Paul, MN: Llewellyn Publications, 1994.

Shandler, Nina. *Estrogen: The Natural Way: Over 250 Easy and Delicious Recipes for Menopause.* New York: Villard Books, 1997.

Sheehy, Gail. *The Silent Passage: Menopause.* Revised and updated. New York: Simon and Schuster, Pocket Books, 1995.

Siguel, Edward N., M.D., Ph.D. *Essential Fatty Acids in Health and Disease.* Brookline, MA: Nutrek Press, 1994.

Theodosakis, Jason, M.D.; Brenda Adderly, M.H.A.; and Barry Fox, Ph.D. *The Arthritis Cure: The Medical Miracle That Can Halt, Reverse, and May Even Cure Osteoarthritis.* New York: St. Martin's Press, 1997.

Thrash, Agatha, M.D. *Eat for Strength: A Vegetarian Cookbook.* Oil-Free edition. Seale, AL: NewLifestyle Books, 1978.

Thrash, Agatha M., M.D.; and Calvin L. Thrash, M.D. *The Animal Connection: Cancer and Other Disease from Animals and Foods of Animal Origin.* Seale, AL: NewLifestyle Books, 1983.

Thrash, Agatha M. M.D.; and Calvin L. Thrash, M.D. *Diabetes and the Hypoglycemic Syndrome: Facts, Findings, and Natural Treatments.* Revised ed. Seale, AL: NewLifestyle Books, 1994.

Thrash, Sue. *Prepublication Excerpts from Distinctive Vegetarian Cuisine: Lively and Appetizing Vegan Cookery*. Seale, AL: NewLifestyle Books, 1992.

Vliet, Elizabeth Lee, M.D. *Screaming to be Heard: Hormonal Connections Women Suspect . . . and Doctors Ignore*. New York: M. Evans and Company, 1995.

Weed, Susun S. *Menopausal Years: The Wise Woman Way*. Woodstock, NY: Ash Tree Publishing, 1992.

Weil, Andrew, M.D. *Ask Dr. Weil: Vitamins and Minerals*. New York: Ivy Books, 1997.

Whitaker, Julian M., M.D. *Dr. Whitaker's Guide to Natural Hormone Replacement*. Potomac, MD: Phillips Publishing, 1997.

Whitaker, Julian M., M.D. *Reversing Diabetes*. New York: Warner Books, 1987.

Whitaker, Julian M., M.D. *Reversing Heart Disease*. New York: Warner Books, 1985.

Wilson, Robert A., M.D. *Feminine Forever*. New York: M. Evans and Company, 1966.

Winter, Ruth, M.S. *A Consumer's Dictionary of Cosmetic Ingredients*. Updated 4th ed. New York: Three Rivers Press, 1994.

Winter, Ruth, M.S. *A Consumer's Dictionary of Food Additives*. Updated 4th ed. New York: Three Rivers Press, 1994.

Wright, Jonathan V., M.D.; and John Morgenthaler. *Natural Hormone Replacement For Women Over Forty-Five*. Petaluma, CA: Smart Publications, 1997.

Consumer Education

Oldways Preservation and Exchange Trust

(25 First St., Cambridge MA 02141; Telephone 617-621-3000)

"Diet and Nutrition: Back to the Future" (reprint from *Encyclopedia Britannica, 1997 Medical and Health Annual*).

"The Healthy Traditional Latin American Diet Pyramid," 1996.

"The Traditional Healthy Asian Diet Pyramid," 1995.

"The Traditional Healthy Mediterranean Diet Pyramid," 1994.

"Vegetarian Diet Pyramid," 1997.

Physicians Committee for Responsible Medicine position papers (5100 Wisconsin Ave. NW, Suite 404, Washington DC 20016; Telephone 202-686-2210)

"Boning Up on Calcium and Osteoporosis"

"Calcium in Plant-Based Diets"

"Cholesterol and Heart Disease"

"Diet and Diabetes"

"Food Choices for Health." Cancer Prevention and Survival Series.

"Food Power for Athletes"

"Foods and Arthritis"

"Foods for Cancer Prevention"

"Hypoglycemia and Diet"

"Milk: No Longer Recommended or Required"

"A Natural Approach to Menopause." Breast Cancer Prevention and Survival Series. Condensed from *Eat Right, Live Longer* by Neal D. Barnard, M.D., Harmony Books, 1995.

"The New Approach to Prostate Problems." By Neal D. Barnard, M.D.

"PCRM Study of Low-Fat, Unrefined Vegan Diet in Treatment of Diabetes."

"Permanent Weight Control"

"The Protein Myth"

"Recommended Readings on Diet and Health"

"Recommended Revisions for *Dietary Guidelines for Americans*"

"Research on the Major Killers of Americans"

"Vegetarian Diets for Children: Right from the Start"

"Vegetarian Diets for Pregnancy"

"Vegetarian Foods: Powerful for Health"

"Vitamin B12 Facts for Vegetarians"

"What's Wrong with Dairy Products?"

Physicians Committee for Responsible Medicine reprints

"Calcium in Foods" J.A.T. Pennington. In *Bowes and Church's Food Values of Portions Commonly Used.* New York: Harper and Row, 1989.

"Nutritional Factors in Menstrual Pain and Premenstrual Syndrome." By Neal D. Barnard, M.D.

"Vitamin B12: A Genuine but Simple Issue." From *Food for Life: How the New Four Food Groups Can Save Your Life* by Neal D. Barnard, M.D., Harmony Books, 1993.

"Women and Cancer: Opportunities for Prevention." By Neal D. Barnard, M.D. Reprint from *PCRM Update,* Sept./Oct. 1991.

Pamphlets

Celiac Disease Foundation. *Guidelines for a Gluten-Free Lifestyle.* 2nd ed. Studio City, CA: Celiac Disease Foundation, 1997.

Oldways Preservation and Exchange Trust. *Avocados, Diet, and Health: Perspectives from Traditional Diets. A Summary Report.* Cambridge, MA: Oldways Preservation and Exchange Trust, 1995.

Oldways Preservation and Exchange Trust. *Changing American Appetites: An Oldways International Symposium.* Boston, MA: Oldways Preservation and Exchange Trust, 1994.

Oldways Preservation and Exchange Trust. *Crete, Greece, and Healthy Mediterranean Diets: An International Symposium.* Cambridge, MA: Oldways Preservation and Exchange Trust, 1997.

Oldways Preservation and Exchange Trust. *Food, Culture, and Discovery: From Columbus to the Twenty-First Century.* Boston, MA: Oldways Preservation and Exchange Trust, 1992.

Oldways Preservation and Exchange Trust. *1997 International Conference on Vegetarian Diets.* Cambridge, MA: Oldways Preservation and Exchange Trust, 1997.

Oldways Preservation and Exchange Trust. *Perspectives from the Mediterranean: Food, Wine, Culture, and Health.* Boston, MA: Oldways Preservation and Exchange Trust, 1993.

Oldways Preservation and Exchange Trust. *Tree Nuts, Health, and the Mediterranean Diet: A Summary Report.* Boston, MA: Oldways Preservation and Exchange Trust, 1994.

Thrash, Agatha M., M.D.; and Calvin L. Thrash, M.D. *The Prostate: A Monograph.* Seale, AL: NewLifestyle Books, 1991.

Magazine Articles

Bloyd-Peshkin, Sharon. "Physician, Know Thy Nutrition." *Vegetarian Times,* February 1993, 48-52.

Solomon, Neil, M.D., Ph.D. "Natural Strategies Can Substitute for Hormone Replacement Therapy (HRT)." *The Experts' Optimal Health Journal,* volume 1, issue 2 (1997), 11.

Newspaper Articles and Press Releases

National Heart, Lung, and Blood Institute. "The Postmenopausal Estrogen/Progestin Interventions (PEPI) Trial." Bethesda, MD: National Heart, Lung, and Blood Institute; National Institutes of Health; Public Health Service; U.S. Department of Health and Human Services. Press release, 17 November 1994.

Brody, Jane. "New Therapy for Menopause Reduces Risks." Reprinted from *New York Times National,* 18 November 1994.

Graedon, Joe and Teresa. "Estrogen Link to Breast Cancer Has Been Confirmed by Research." *Hendersonville (NC) Times-News,* 17 June 1998, p. 6C.

Index

G

H

We welcome comments from our readers. Feel free to write to us at the following address:

Editorial Department
Huntington House Publishers
P.O. Box 53788
Lafayette, LA 70505

―――――――――――――――

More Good Books from Huntington House Publishers

The Eagle's Claw
Christians and the IRS
by Steve Richardson

The Eagle's Claw, based on the author's experience as a CPA defending Christians and Christian organizations from IRS attacks, helps Christians understand the IRS. The IRS makes mistakes, sometimes huge mistakes. Richardson provides appropriate defensive tools to fight back. Some of these attacks were unjustified and some, in his view, were illegal and designed to limit the actions and activities of the Church in our society. In fact, the author states, some of these IRS attacks appear to be motivated by a partisan political agenda.

ISBN 1-56384-128-2

The Slash Brokers
by Jeff S. Barganier

The gruesome but overwhelming evidence is in. The Chinese Communists are secretly involved in the lucrative harvesting of human body parts and fetus consumption.

ISBN 1-56384-150-9

Communism the Cold War, & the FBI Connection
by Herman O. Bly

One out of four people in the world live under Communist rule. If Americans think they are safe from the "red plague," they'd better think again, says author Herman Bly. He will reveal what he's learned in years of counter-intelligence work, and how our country is being lulled into a false sense of security.

ISBN 1-56384-149-5

Dark Cures
Have Doctors Lost Their Ethics?
by Paul deParrie

When traditional ethics were the standard in the field of medicine, one could take comfort in the knowledge that doctors and medical institutions put the health and well-being of the patient above all else. Today, however, pagan ethics have pervaded the professions once properly called "the healing arts, " turning doctors into social engineers and petty gods, and patients into unwitting guinea pigs.

ISBN 1-56384-099-5

Spiritual Warfare
The Invisible Invasion
by Thomas R. Horn

Thomas Horn illustrates through fresh and powerful new insights that while demonic activity has frequently been overlooked, the close collaboration between social architects and ancient evil powers has at times allowed demons to control the machine of world governments, and the moral and social trends of a nation.

ISBN 1-56384-129-0

One Last Call
A Guide for the
Achievement of Lasting Peace
by Donnell L. Harris

One Last Call is a prescription for action to make a better future for ourselves and the generations to come. It is also an invitation to join a serious movement of peace, which will carry us into the 21st century. Now is the time to return order and vitality to our social health. For too long, the social body has been under attack, eaten away by the corrosive cancers of chauvinism, bigotry, prejudice, and hate. You cannot legislate the cure. The new millennium offers a great opportunity for a new start.

ISBN 0-933451-39-3

Make Yourself Ready
Preparing to Meet the King
by Harland Miller

Instead of trying to convince readers that one doctrinal position is more valid than another, *Make Yourself Ready* was written to help Christians prepare for the Second Coming. By analyzing Old Testament events, Miller explains how we can avoid Lucifer's age-old deceptions. Scripturally sound and eminently inspiring, *Make Yourself Ready* will create newfound excitement for the return of the Hope of Heaven and show readers how to become truly ready for Judgment Day.

ISBN 0-933451-36-9

Christian Revolution: Practical Answers to Welfare and Addiction
by Arthur Pratt

In *Christian Revolution: Practical Answers to Welfare and Addiction*, Pratt demonstrates that real social and political change starts with radical honesty about the nature of the problem. He has called for Congressional action based on his own scientific evidence in the treatment of addiction. He affirms a renewed faith in Jesus Christ as the inspiration for such action, seeing the church as a servant of our country, not a mentor.

ISBN 1-56384-143-6